The Elements of Education for School Leaders

What skills are needed to ensure success as a school leader today? How do you ensure great teaching and learning is happening in your school? How do you build leadership capacity within your teams? To answer these questions, the authors combined up-to-date research with their own leadership experiences to assemble fifty essential principles that will help school leaders focus on what is most important.

This book provides clear, concise, and valuable advice for school leaders and their leadership teams. Each principle is paired with a case study that places each one in a real-life context. *The Elements of Education for School Leaders* is an essential resource for anyone who wants to lead an effective school.

Julia Chun is the director of global education at Avenues The World School. She also was the founding principal of the New Visions Charter High School for Advanced Math and Science, the first in a network of ten charter high schools in New York City.

Tyler Tingley has led four American independent schools: Kingswood-Oxford School in Connecticut, the Blake School in Minnesota, and Phillips Exeter Academy in New Hampshire, as well as being co-head of Avenues The World School in New York City. He is currently a strategic advisor at Avenues The World School.

William Lidwell is the chief research and development officer of the Tiger Works research and development team at Avenues The World School. He is the author of several books, including the best-selling *Universal Principles of Design*.

T0386348

**Also Available from
Routledge Eye On Education**
(www.routledge.com/k-12)

The Elements of Education for Teachers:
50 Research-Based Principles Every Educator Should Know
Austin Volz, Julia Higdon, and William Lidwell

The Elements of Education for Curriculum Designers:
50 Research-Based Principles Every Educator Should Know
Rebecca Strauss, Austin Volz, and William Lidwell

What Great Teachers Do Differently, 3e:
Nineteen Things That Matter Most
Todd Whitaker

What Great Principals Do Differently, 3e:
Twenty Things That Matter Most
Todd Whitaker

Essential Truths for Principals
Danny Steele and Todd Whitaker

Principal Bootcamp:
Accelerated Strategies to Influence and Lead from Day One
Brad Johnson

The Elements of Education for School Leaders

50 Research-Based Principles Every School Leader Should Know

Julia Chun, Tyler Tingley, and William Lidwell

Routledge
Taylor & Francis Group

NEW YORK AND LONDON

First published 2023
by Routledge
605 Third Avenue, New York, NY 10158

and by Routledge
4 Park Square, Milton Park, Abingdon, Oxon, OX14 4RN

Routledge is an imprint of the Taylor & Francis Group, an informa business

© 2023 Taylor & Francis

The right of Julia Chun, Tyler Tingley, and William Lidwell to be
identified as authors of this work has been asserted in accordance with
sections 77 and 78 of the Copyright, Designs and Patents Act 1988.

All rights reserved. No part of this book may be reprinted or
reproduced or utilised in any form or by any electronic, mechanical,
or other means, now known or hereafter invented, including
photocopying and recording, or in any information storage or retrieval
system, without permission in writing from the publishers.

Trademark notice: Product or corporate names may be trademarks
or registered trademarks, and are used only for identification and
explanation without intent to infringe.

Library of Congress Cataloging-in-Publication Data
Names: Chun, Julia, author. | Tingley, Tyler, author. | Lidwell,
   William, author.
Title: The elements of education for school leaders : 50 research-based
   principles every leader should know / Julia Chun, Tyler Tingley, and
   William Lidwell.
Description: New York, NY : Routledge, 2023. | Series: Routledge eye
   on education | Includes bibliographical references.
Identifiers: LCCN 2022036656 | ISBN 9780367337483 (hardback) |
   ISBN 9780367337476 (paperback) | ISBN 9780429321641 (ebook)
Subjects: LCSH: Educational leadership. | School management and
   organization. | Educational leadership—Case studies. | School
   management and organization—Case studies.
Classification: LCC LB2806 .C45 2023 | DDC 371.2/011—dc23/
   eng/20220922
LC record available at https://lccn.loc.gov/2022036656

ISBN: 978-0-367-33748-3 (hbk)
ISBN: 978-0-367-33747-6 (pbk)
ISBN: 978-0-429-32164-1 (ebk)

DOI: 10.4324/9780429321641

Typeset in Palatino
by Apex CoVantage, LLC

Dedicated to
Stephen and Insook Chun
Avery and Arabella Rhodes
Chad Vignola
Marcia M. Tingley

Contents

Acknowledgments

The authors would like to thank many people who have made this work possible.

Chad Vignola: for his patience, wisdom, and the bottomless cups of tea during the writing process. Avery and Arabella Rhodes: for providing the inspiration to be better today than yesterday. Stephen and Insook Chun: for their encouragement to always work hard and be humble.

For the many friends and colleagues who have given us so many models of excellent school leadership on which to draw.

We are grateful to our incredible colleagues at Avenues The World School who provided us with both direct and indirect support as we worked to bring this book into existence. Thank you especially to Marcia Tingley, Aniella Day, Rebecca Strauss, Julia Higdon, Jeff Clark, and all the members of the R&D team.

Finally, we would like to thank everyone at Routledge for their patience, professionalism, and support of this book.

Meet the Authors

Julia Chun is the director of global education at Avenues The World School. Prior to this, she served as upper-division head at the Avenues New York campus, leading faculty, students, and families in grades 6–12. She also was the founding principal of the New Visions Charter High School for Advanced Math and Science, the first in a network of ten charter high schools in New York City. Julia earned a master's degree in English literature from Columbia University, a master's degree in educational leadership from Teachers College, and a bachelor's degree in English literature from the University of Chicago.

Tyler Tingley has led four American independent schools: Kingswood-Oxford School in Connecticut, the Blake School in Minnesota, Phillips Exeter Academy in and New Hampshire, as well as being co-head of Avenues The World School in New York City. He is currently a strategic advisor at Avenues The World School. He holds an AB in English from Harvard College and a EdM and EdD from the Harvard Graduate School of Education.

William Lidwell is the chief research and development officer of the Tiger Works research and development team at Avenues The World School. He is the author of several books, including the best-selling *Universal Principles of Design*.

Introduction

Being a school leader is arguably both the most fulfilling and most rewarding job in education. However, it can also be the most thankless and lonely one. The dichotomous nature of the role makes the position challenging, as school leadership requires a unique set of skills and traits that are often diametrically opposed—one must be an instructional technician who can analyze the precise details of a classroom as well as a broad generalist who can communicate big-picture goals to the various constituencies in the school.

Given the challenges inherent in the role, this book is intended to be a quick reference tool for leaders who need immediate assistance but don't have ample time to sift through complex texts or lengthy articles. It can be considered a troubleshooting guide for leaders who need to get pertinent information and practical advice on a topic without having to do the research themselves. It is also intended to inspire school leaders when they need to make tough decisions and untangle seemingly intractable problems, as we understand what you are facing, having been there ourselves.

The format of the book is simple. We have chosen fifty leadership principles that are the most essential for any school leader to understand. The list is not meant to be comprehensive; it represents the most common—but often the most misunderstood—principles in school leadership. Each chapter is double-sided; the left side defines the principle, providing the most current research and offering expert advice. The right side presents a case study, with a familiar cast of characters in a school that may be similar to your own. The case study is meant to contextualize the issue, provide a narrative that brings the principle to light, and embed it in a real-world scenario. All characters in the case studies are fictional.

We anticipate some educators may find this book useful in leading a professional-development workshop or continuing education for those who are running schools or hope someday to do so. If this is your need, we suggest you follow this plan:

Pick case studies that illustrate the principles of leadership on which you are focused.

Ask the participants to summarize what has taken place.

Ask the participants to suggest alternative scenarios to the actions of the administrators of North High.

Evaluate those scenarios to see which ones best exemplify the principle explained on the page to the left of the case study.

The book will be at its most useful if leaders can lean on it much as they would an experienced consultant. The idea is not to read the book from cover to cover but to refer to the chapters as topics become relevant. We have poured much of our collective school leadership years into these principles and case studies, and we hope you can benefit from our experience.

Julia Chun
Tyler Tingley
William Lidwell

1 Admissions

The student selection and enrollment process

The most important thing a school leader can do is to partner with the school's admissions director to ensure the school enrolls students who are a "good fit" for the institution. What constitutes a "good fit" will depend on the school's philosophy and the organization's ability to connect to students and families who fit the school's profile. A school leader can support the school's admissions effort in three main ways:

1. Ensuring engagement
2. Supporting understanding
3. Advocating for diversity

A leader should encourage the entire school community to facilitate the admissions process, making admissions and enrollment a priority for the school. The leader should emphasize the importance of administration, faculty, and students attending open houses, volunteering to guide tours, and helping at school information and recruitment sessions. When prospective families visit the school, faculty should welcome visitors into their classrooms, while students should be able to articulate the school's strengths and unique features as well as their personal experiences attending the school.

Admissions officers often have a cursory understanding of curricular details and lack the pedagogical experience to be able to advocate particular courses or activities to an outside audience. Teachers may be reluctant to volunteer to offer additional time to the admissions effort, and it is sometimes challenging to ask them to take on more responsibilities. Leaders should utilize their professional-duty system to enroll teachers to support the admissions and enrollment team. They can then ask the faculty volunteers to help the admissions team understand how to best describe classes and other school offerings.

Leaders should partner with admissions directors to make diversity and equity in the admissions and enrollment process a key priority. Research shows that racially and socioeconomically diverse schools cultivate students with higher test scores, increased college attendance, and improved critical-thinking skills. A diverse group of faculty should attend recruitment fairs and school information sessions as ambassadors. In addition, schools can also intentionally reduce barriers to enrollment in multiple ways: by creating promotional materials in multiple languages, having school representatives who speak languages other than English available to answer questions, and providing child care at information sessions and school lotteries.

See also   Community Engagement, Inclusivity and Diversity, School Culture

RESOURCES

Anderson, Melinda D. "The Promise of Integrated Schools." *The Atlantic*, February 16, 2016.

The New Schools Venture Fund. *Creating an Intentionally Diverse School: Lessons Learned.* Oakland, CA: New Schools Venture Fund Report, October 2017.

DOI: 10.4324/9780429321641-1

CASE STUDY

North High School, a school of 1,200 students in grades nine through twelve, didn't have any trouble filling the seats in its classrooms, but Jim Short, the principal, was still interested in admissions. To Short, the admissions process represented one of the key ways North could communicate with the parents and potential students in its neighborhood. "All the newspapers want to report is bad news," Short complained to his administrative team. "Some kid gets caught shoplifting and they put it on the front page. A student wins the state science fair and it's buried in the middle of the paper. If we want parents to know what we do well, we've got to take responsibility for getting that story out."

Short met with the district's admissions officer, Linda Walker, who oversaw admissions at North and two other schools. "I want North to have an admissions fair," Short said. "I want the kids to make exhibits of all the things they like and the school does well. I want our glee club and pep band to perform. I want to introduce the captains of the debate team and the sports teams. I want our current parents to come and get to know the potential new parents and tell them about their own experience at North. I want those parents to bring their own students to welcome the new students. And most of all, I want our potential families of color to feel welcomed and safe."

"That sounds like a great idea, Jim," said Linda Walker. "But there's no way I can organize that. I'll support the idea and take care of mailing lists, but you've got to plan the fair on your own."

"We'll organize it," Short replied.

At the next faculty meeting, Short asked for volunteers to help plan and execute the admissions fair. He made it clear it was a high priority for faculty to attend. He appointed several volunteers to organize the student groups that would be featured and the students who would speak. He met with the leaders of the student council and got their support for getting the student body to be ambassadors for North. And he met with the parent council and got their enthusiastic support for the project.

"Everyone wants the community to recognize the quality of North," Short said. "And everybody has a personal stake in making sure families come ready to support the values that make North a good school."

2 Assessment

Understanding student performance and progress

While all tests are assessments, not all assessments are tests. Assessment can refer to everything from standardized state and national tests to in-class projects, exams, quizzes, and portfolios, as well as more informal assessments of knowledge like daily "exit tickets" assessing students' understanding of the day's lesson. Leaders should ensure the school is utilizing various types of assessment, both to provide individual students with feedback on their progress and to allow faculty to analyze patterns of student performance in order to improve instruction.

Summative assessments such as state tests can be reliable and broad indicators of how a student, grade, class, or school is faring academically and to identify trends in student learning. Most schools utilize summative assessment data to create intervention systems for students and to plan professional development for teachers. However, researchers have found a curriculum-embedded formative assessment system has the greatest impact on student learning (just below having an excellent classroom teacher). Accordingly, leaders should also support a schoolwide system of formative assessment. The system should incorporate the intended curriculum standards the school has chosen to adopt (i.e., the International Baccalaureate, Common Core, etc.). School leaders should also provide ample opportunities for faculty and leadership to review and understand the data from these assessments and plan the implementation of corrective measures in their classrooms.

The goal of summative assessments is to evaluate students' performance at a given time against a benchmark. Summative assessments lag student achievement and are ways to determine whether students have learned the content and skills expected of them. Usually, this occurs at the end of an instructional unit or break point in the school year. The goal of formative assessment, on the other hand, is to understand where a student is in their learning process to inform ongoing instruction. Formative assessments can be in the moment. A typical formative assessment could be an end-of-teaching-period exit ticket in which the student demonstrates whether they mastered a single lesson. Formative assessments, when used appropriately, allow for early intervention and can provide students with useful feedback to take action in their own learning. The public often focuses on summative results—but far more important is the school's system of assessment *for* learning, which is formative assessment.

See also Curriculum Leadership, Grading

RESOURCES

Hattie, John. *Visible Learning*. New York, NY: Routledge, 2012.

Stiggins, Rick J. *An Introduction to Student-Involved Assessment for Learning*, 5th ed. London, England: Pearson/Merrill Prentice Hall, 2008.

Wiliam, Dylan. *Embedded Formative Assessment*, 2nd ed. Bloomington, IN: Solution Tree Press, 2017.

DOI: 10.4324/9780429321641-2

CASE STUDY

The school year at North High generally ended with students taking a number of state-designed comprehensive exams in foundational subjects such as English and math. Jim Short and his academic team of department heads studied the results of the state exams closely. The cumulative results were often published in the local paper and could, if the scores were significantly lower than in previous years, be a source of parental concern. Short and his team were more interested in the breakdown of the scores by grade and subject, since these scores could give clues to weaknesses in North's curriculum and instruction. But Short was careful how this analysis was used. He knew the limits that "teaching to the test" could bring, and he wanted to make sure his faculty didn't think scores on the state exams were the only performance indices that mattered.

"Let's talk about formative testing," Short said to his department heads in one of their pre-school meetings. "How much do you talk about that in your department meetings?"

"Not much," replied Dick Brown, the chair of the math department. "We're generally bogged down with student issues—performance issues with kids who aren't getting the material. It's a continuous battle."

"Exactly," said Genevieve Weber, the chair of modern languages. "We spend all our time talking about kids who are doing poorly."

There were nods of agreement around the room.

"Well, that's exactly the reason I raised the subject of formative testing," Short said. "A good formative test is both diagnostic and educational. Kids learn by figuring things out, and a formative test asks the kids to figure out material they haven't yet fully learned. It's not a test to find the holes in the students' learning. That's what the state exams do. It's to help them build their skills while seeing where they're having trouble learning.

"For example," Short continued, "suppose the kids are having trouble factoring polynomials. The teacher can see that in class, so on the weekly quiz, she puts a couple of problems that include some of the first steps in performing the operation. The kids can use those problems to help them figure out the harder problems and learn in the process.

"I don't know enough Spanish to give you a good example, Genevieve," Short went on. "But the principle of formative testing is the same in every discipline. Have your faculty experiment with thinking about the majority of their tests as a learning experience. It will help if you have some department meetings where faculty write test questions collectively and help each other out. And in the end, we should see the results of formative testing in our state scores."

3   Attendance

Being present for learning

If students don't show up for classes, the school is failing to meet the most basic standard of performance. Research shows that students who are chronically absent from school (more than fifteen days a year) are more likely to perform below grade level academically and are four times as likely to drop out of school. Furthermore, school absenteeism correlates to poor outcomes in adulthood—from poverty to adverse health effects to increased involvement in the criminal justice system.

A robust attendance system is essential to knowing which students are chronically absent, which are most at risk, and how best to intervene to ensure they come to school. Taking daily attendance is mandatory for all schools, and tracking student attendance to identify which students are absent and creating interventions for them is crucial. Often, the mere fact that the school reaches out to notify the parent or guardian about missed days of school will result in better attendance. Also, having an administrator or attendance coordinator do a home visit for students who are chronically absent can mitigate the problem. Identifying the issue behind why the child is missing school and addressing it directly is key. Schools can also generate morning reminder calls or create a buddy system to encourage better school attendance. Incentives for good school attendance (awards, privileges, prizes) can also help boost attendance.

An engaging school curriculum makes a significant difference in whether students attend school regularly. If students are excited about learning and feel the content in their classes has a real-world application, they are more likely to come to school. Schools should offer classes that support both college-bound students and those who want to enter a technical trade after high school. By offering art, music, dance, or sports, a school can attract students who have interests other than purely academic ones.

Students who build meaningful relationships with people at school attend school more frequently. These can be with classmates, teachers, teammates, or a mentor. School leaders should ensure all students are connected with a faculty advisor, who should monitor their advisees' absences and reach out to a student with a pattern of missed school days. Similarly, the school must partner with families of students who have attendance issues. Parents and guardians can often shed light on why the student is missing school—whether it's due to a safety, scheduling, or physical or mental health issue. Once the reason for missing school is identified, the school can create an intervention plan to help the student get back on track and in school regularly.

See also   Differentiation, School Climate

RESOURCES

Roderick, Melissa, Thomas Kelley-Kemple, David W. Johnson, and Nicole O. Beechum. *Research Summary: Preventable Failure Improvements in Long-Term Outcomes When High Schools Focused on the Ninth Grade Year*. Chicago, IL: University of Chicago Consortium on Chicago School Research, 2014.

US Department of Education. *Chronic Absenteeism in the Nation's Schools*. Washington, DC: US Department of Education, 2016.

DOI: 10.4324/9780429321641-3

CASE STUDY

The opening faculty meeting of the year was always a special time for the faculty and administrative staff of North High. Just as many students couldn't sleep the night before the first day of school, the faculty experienced similar anticipation at the start of a new year. Recognizing the heightened attention that went with this anticipation, Jim Short always chose the first faculty meeting to deliver a message he thought was critically important.

"Over the course of this meeting and this school year," Short began, "we'll spend a lot of time talking about how to make our students' experiences better. We'll discuss programs to improve and new programs to start. But we need to remember that no program—new or old—will make a difference if the kids don't come to school. It sounds simplistic, but nothing is more important than attendance. That's our first job—to make sure the students show up in our classes.

"I can't emphasize this enough. The vast majority of you will be student advisors this year. You need to be aware of your advisees' attendance. If a student is out of school for three days, you need to call home and talk to their parents. That will probably mean an evening call. I'm sorry for that; but we know that talking to parents directly often solves an attendance issue. And if the student is seriously ill or there's family trouble, we have resources to help. If you have trouble reaching a family, the dean's office can help. I've told parents in my pre-school letter that we'll be calling if their children aren't in school. They'll expect us to follow up.

"Often, the reason a student misses school," Short continued, "has to do with conditions in the school that are our responsibility. If a student doesn't feel safe, if they are teased or bullied, they'll find lots of ways to escape those uncomfortable situations. Likewise, if they're lost in class, if they can't understand the language, if their educational background hasn't prepared them for the lessons we ask them to learn, they'll try to opt out. That's where they really need us as faculty. We need to find the ways to make North High a place the students really want to attend.

"Ultimately," Short concluded, "attendance issues often come down to the relationship of a student and their family to people at the school. If your advisee knows you well and trusts you, there's a good chance they'll come and tell you if they're getting bullied. And if the family knows you, they might initiate a call if they perceive something going wrong in their child's life."

Kearney, Christopher A., David Heyne, and Carolina Gonzálvez. "Editorial: School Attendance and Problematic School Absenteeism in Youth." *Frontiers in Psychology* 11 (November 6, 2020): 602242. https://doi.org/10.3389/fpsyg.2020.602242.

4   Change Management

A coordinated process to create lasting change

It is well established in the business world that without effective change processes, it is impossible for companies to compete and succeed. Schools, however, have not always pursued this standard. Most schools still embrace a centuries-old model that prioritizes compliance and replication rather than one that emphasizes understanding and innovation.

When a school employs a systematic approach to change, the change is much more likely to be meaningful and enduring. However, change without guidance and planning can result in poor student outcomes, a disgruntled faculty, and a chaotic school climate. When leading change in schools, it is helpful to think about change in three phases:

1. Design
2. Transfer
3. Implementation

In the design phase, the school must establish a clear purpose that aligns with the school's mission and vision. The purpose could originate with the leadership team or innovators within the school. School leaders should view their primary role as champions of change, as motivation will be an important contributor to success during the design phase. This phase will also be the time to clarify the specifics for the planned change. The change team leadership, time frame, budget, and project goals should be clearly articulated and defined during the design phase.

In the transfer phase, leadership must communicate to all stakeholders an authentic and urgent need for change. However, some caution should be exercised lest school leaders create a "burning platform" scenario. Once the need for change is communicated, an influential team of innovators can be assembled to lead the change initiative. Leaders should support this effort by helping to cultivate a positive environment for change—for example, restructuring school hierarchies, removing barriers, or recognition and rewards for people who make the change happen. The innovators will need to define what success looks like and get buy-in to that goal from the school community.

In the implementation phase of change management, school leaders should think deeply about schoolwide acceptance of change and how to assess the progress and alignment to the school's strategic objectives. It will be important to do this by gathering feedback from the school community, reflecting, and iterating to improve the original design. Leaders should recognize that the rate of change adoption will follow a classic S-curve pattern, with innovators and early adopters supporting the change first, followed by late adopters and finally laggards. Leaders should expect the change process will be slow to start, will be messy, and will not progress in a linear way.

See also   Innovation Leadership, Prioritization

RESOURCES

Deming, W. Edwards. *Out of the Crisis*. Cambridge, MA: Massachusetts Institute of Technology, Center for Advanced Engineering Study, 1986.

DOI: 10.4324/9780429321641-4

CASE STUDY

It was exam season at North High, and Jim Short walked into the cafeteria to see how the morning exams were going. This morning, American history had most of the eleventh grade bent over their blue books, struggling to construct short essays on a long list of topics that appeared to be Xerox copies of once-mimeographed sheets composed decades earlier. "Why do we test this way?" Short thought, as he reflected on how the morning's news regarding climate change and global pandemic described a world far different from that assumed in the tried-and-true tests the students were completing.

Short had had that thought before, and when he returned to his office, he wrote notes for a study group "to prepare a recommendation for substituting group projects for evaluation and credit *in place* of final exams." Over the next few weeks, working with his senior staff and the academic department chairs, he convened a representative group to study the issue and make a recommendation.

Once the study group was established, Short spent a good deal of time with them to help them understand why he thought the question was significant. In particular, he asked them to talk to students and to professors at the local colleges to see if well-designed group projects might not be more useful academic training than traditional exams. He also arranged to have the group meet with the parent council and hear their thoughts.

Short could see that this issue could become very political, with faculty factions lobbying for or against the changes under discussion. He told the study group he wanted the group to present the arguments for and against the proposed change, and then he and his senior staff would make the final decision after a full faculty discussion.

He also told the study group he would not *require* the changes they proposed but would seek volunteers to test the new proposal. He was frank in admitting he didn't expect a great number to embrace the change at the start; but he did expect those who did to do so enthusiastically and that the enthusiastic response of the students would at least equal the faculty enthusiasm.

Kotter, John P. *Leading Change*. Boston, MA: Harvard Business School Press, 1986.

Savitz, Eric. "CEO's 'Burning Platform' Memo Highlights Nokia's Woes." *Forbes* 53 (February 2011).

5 College Counseling

Guidance and support for students in the college application and admissions process

College counseling is one component to building a strong academic culture at the school. However, it is not merely a transactional endeavor but a product of a long-term relationship. While there is a results-oriented dimension to college counseling, it should be viewed as much more than just ensuring a student gains admission into a college. College counseling is a process that supports students in finding out (or at least starting to think about and plan around) their interests, where they see themselves in the future, and a means to achieving their goals. If viewed this way, college counseling should start in ninth grade. College admissions should be looked at as an important product of the college counseling process—but only one of the outcomes. The larger goal should be to support students in preparation for adulthood and guide them in the options that will best position them for future success.

School leaders should ensure all students receive guidance from a college counselor on what courses to take and on their academic performance and, as senior year approaches, create with them a curated list of schools or certification programs, or both, to which to apply. Counselors should assist students in identifying scholarships and arranging interviews and college visits, as well as regularly meeting with students to ensure they are staying on track to complete their applications on time. Leaders should work to get the effective ratio of students to counselors as low as possible. The national average of public school students to college counselors is 464:1. Most independent high schools offer a forty- to sixty-student-to-counselor ratio. As these numbers suggest, students who attend private institutions have the distinct advantage of more college counseling support than their public school peers. Strategies that leaders can use to bring this ratio down are to train other faculty (i.e., teachers and guidance counselors) to take on some college counseling responsibilities or to partner with a graduate school of education to bring college counseling interns to the school.

To ensure all students receive guidance, it is important that the school offer a class to help students set postsecondary goals and build pathways to reach them. This class can be a dedicated college counseling class or part of a larger advisory program; however, it should have a college preparation curriculum that attends to goal setting, communication skills, and the college research and application process.

See also Mission and Vision

RESOURCES

The Education Trust. School Counselors Matter. *The Education Trust*, February 2019.

DOI: 10.4324/9780429321641-5

CASE STUDY

The practice of college counseling had changed significantly in the days since Jim Short was a student. Not only had the number of applicants for competitive colleges increased dramatically, the place of college in the lives of young people had also changed. Going to college had always meant a student was likely to earn more income over their lifetime and often enjoy the opportunity of more interesting work. Today, those factors were intensified and complicated by students who represented much greater racial, social, and income diversity than Short had encountered in his youth. That meant the place of college advising was central to the education North High provided.

Short was concerned his college counselors could not handle the workload his staffing parameters dictated. He knew that local private schools generally had their college counselors handle no more than fifty students, working with them in an intensifying relationship from ninth to twelfth grade. North's counselors had hundreds of counselees and often wrote more than 300 college letters of recommendation a year. The private school counselors really knew their students and spoke with authority about their accomplishments. His counselors were overwhelmed with the writing load and often resorted to brief, formulaic letters of recommendation.

Short started meeting regularly with the college counseling team to hear their concerns. He suggested that he recruit and the counseling staff train a group of volunteer faculty to help work with the younger students. He wasn't surprised when there was an enthusiastic response from the faculty. Volunteer faculty worked with the students in grades nine and ten, handling them over in grade eleven to members of the counseling staff. Faculty provided background material for college recommendations, and many followed their advisees informally right through to graduation.

The volunteer counselors also had an impact on the culture of the school. They saw the stress the students were under as they faced college admissions, as well as the importance of this process in their lives. In the past, many faculty saw college admissions as somebody else's problem. Now the volunteer involvement meant more faculty understood this was a shared cultural responsibility. Short saw no end to the pressure on college admissions, but sharing the burden improved the experience for both the counselors and especially for the students of North.

6 Communication Excellence

Conveying a combination of vision, empathy, and expertise

Effective school leaders must write impeccably, speak professionally, and be a warm and dynamic in-person presence in the school community. They are the face of the organization, and they model how people should communicate and treat one another in school. The standard they set creates a tone for the culture of the school.

Writing well is arguably the most important communication skill school leaders must possess. School leaders communicate through writing on a daily basis—everything from faculty newsletters to parent correspondence to school yearbook introductions. It is the primary way leaders stay connected to students, faculty, and parents. All written correspondence should be grammatically correct and free from error. It is helpful to have another person, a trusted colleague, proofread and check the tenor and tone of all writing. They should edit for grammatical errors and ensure the writing is free from politically biased rhetoric or inappropriate language. One spelling error, grammatical mistake, or misused phrase may seem like a small issue, but any misstep is unacceptable, as stakeholders often equate the professional merit and integrity of the leader to how well they compose a correspondence.

Leaders should also practice public speaking, rehearsing and practicing their presentations out loud before delivery. This may require recording a speech, listening to it while taking notes, and making appropriate adjustments. While it may be tempting to read a prepared speech out loud verbatim, it is better to create note cards with a summary of important points, as this enables the leader to make eye contact with the audience and prevents the speech from sounding stilted and rote. The leader may need to take a class on public speaking or employ a coach to assist them in becoming a more proficient public speaker.

Leaders must practice in-person communication. As a school leader, they model how to behave in meetings with stakeholders and students and set the tone for professionalism in the school. Effective listening is key to in-person communication. Leaders must listen carefully and allow the person speaking to be heard. This does not mean they must always agree with the person or act on everything they request. Instead, use the moment as an opportunity to connect, express empathy, and understand the other person's viewpoint. Also be aware of body language when speaking. It can be clear a leader's focus is elsewhere if they are checking their phone or laptop or not looking directly at the person speaking. Likewise, physical manifestations of the leader's displeasure or distress—through body posture or facial expressions—can be at best off-putting and at worst threatening to those around them.

See also   Prioritization, School Climate

RESOURCES

Allensworth, Elaine, James Sebastian, and Molly Gordon. "Principal Leadership Practices, Organizational Improvement, and Student Achievement." Chap. 13 in *Exploring Principal Development and Teacher Outcomes: How Principals Can Strengthen Instruction, Teacher Retention, and Student Achievement*, edited by Peter Youngs, Jihyun Kim, and Madeline Mavrogordato. New York, NY: Routledge, 2020.

DOI: 10.4324/9780429321641-6

CASE STUDY

Jim Short looked at his calendar with a sense of resignation. It was a three meeting day, and each meeting was a command performance. First, he was meeting with the student council over lunch. The subject was, in fact, the menu in the dining hall, a perennial source of student criticism. After school, he had a faculty meeting, and he knew there would be a contentious conversation about the outcome of a recent discipline case. And in the evening, it was the parent council, an important group to keep supportive and involved. Short knew that at one level, his performance was a symbol for school quality, and he needed to be prepared for these three meetings.

The meeting that worried him the least was the parent council. Short invested a lot of time crafting informative and appropriately upbeat newsletters for the parents and faculty and staff. His assistant had been an English major in college. She was an excellent editor and proofed all of Short's writing. He didn't expect any surprises at the parent council meeting.

Even though he knew he would hear complaints, Short looked forward to the student council lunch. Talking to the kids was fun. Short concentrated on speaking to them as if they were adults. He also made it a point to give them his full attention. Nothing lost the students faster than taking a phone call during the meeting. Short worked hard to know every student's name and to listen carefully, even when the subject—such as a request for french fries at every meal—seemed less important.

The faculty could try his patience. There had been a messy discipline case that Short and his discipline committee had decided as best they could. They had opted for leniency in the face of weak evidence. But some faculty thought they had been too easy, and Short anticipated there might be angry words at the meeting. He prepared himself to be calm. His leadership style was based on trying to understand all the factors that went into a decision and then making that decision dispassionately. He wanted to be sure he projected that reasonableness at the faculty meeting.

The faculty meeting went better than he expected, and Short grabbed a quick dinner with the leaders of the parent council before their meeting. He always found it useful to share his agenda with that group in advance to gauge their reaction. Tonight, there were no surprises, and Short enjoyed talking about North High's recent academic and athletic successes with a supportive parent group.

Bredeson, Paul V. "Communications as a Measure of Leadership in Schools: A Portraiture of School Principals." *The High School Journal* 71, no. 4 (April–May 1988): 178–86. www.jstor.org/stable/40364902.

7 Community Engagement

Purposeful partnerships between schools, families, and the community

Research has shown that community engagement leads to improved academic and behavioral outcomes for all students and also increases communication and activism among community groups. School leaders should invest in cultivating these partnerships to:

1. Enhance teaching and learning
2. Strengthen the curriculum
3. Build civic leadership and responsibility

It is important that schools leverage community resources so teaching and learning can be enhanced. Community engagement promotes a school climate that connects students to a broader community. Partnership organizations often have resources that students can access and provide opportunities for students to learn before school, after school, and during the summer. Community engagement can also help students build social capital. Schools that work with community organizations create social networks that support learning and create opportunities for young people.

Community engagement can improve a school's curriculum and curricular offerings. Many schools have academic programs that emphasize engaging and authentic problem-solving. Partnerships with community organizations facilitate the creation of an enacted curriculum that can connect what students are learning in school with the real world. School leaders should leverage outside experts and volunteers to bring their skills and talents to enhance the school's curriculum and support faculty in the classroom. Furthermore, schools that are connected to social services agencies in the community should partner to create continuity across early childhood development and after-school programs to further nurture students' growth and development. School leaders can strengthen family connections by offering parenting, language, and health classes that support parents, siblings, and guardians. This also has the added benefit of increasing family communication and comfort with school, further supporting students' success.

Community engagement provides an authentic way for students to learn about the issues that face the community and creates opportunities for them to voice their opinions and participate in local politics and decision-making. Schools should support students' understanding of civil discourse and what it means to engage with those whose perspectives differ from their own. Schools can also work to advocate for and amplify issues that are important and central to the community's interests. Community engagement allows students to gain confidence to attend and speak up at public meetings, as well as to vote for important issues and support public officials who can make a difference in their neighborhoods. Moreover, schools and community organizations can work together to design solutions to local problems, such as creating a community garden, creating an open and shared learning space, or designing a course to be offered to the community at large.

See also   Communication Excellence, Curriculum Leadership, School Climate

DOI: 10.4324/9780429321641-7

CASE STUDY

Like many public schools, North High allowed its facilities to be used by a wide range of community groups that petitioned the district office to gain permission to use the campus. Jim Short was used to working late and leaving his office to find the local Boy Scout troop in the gymnasium, a community meeting in the auditorium, and other organizations occupying various classrooms.

One day, as he was leaving late again, a woman he knew to be the mother of one of his ninth-graders stopped him in the hall. "Mr. Short," she said, "I'm Grace Anderson, parent of Jimmy. I was here for a Democratic Club block meeting and saw you leave your office. Can I walk with you to your car?"

"Sure," Short replied, "but I warn you, I'm late for dinner, and I'll walk fast." "I'll jog!" Ms. Anderson replied. "One question: Have you ever heard of the Weekend Academy?"

"I think so," Short said. "A Saturday program for grades one through eight?"

"That's right, and we need a home. We've been meeting in the Baptist Church for ten years, and we've grown too big for that facility."

"Call me tomorrow," Short said. "I'm interested."

When Ms. Anderson called the next morning, Short talked to her for half an hour. By the end of the conversation, he was impressed. The program had 450 students enrolled, and they spent a full six-hour day in the Weekend Academy every week. The curriculum was enrichment and some remedial skills for the kids who had missed school or moved around a great deal. Volunteers, including some of his own faculty and a number of his parents, staffed it.

"I'd be very interested in supporting your proposal to the district to base the Weekend Academy at North High," Short told Ms. Anderson, "as long as you let us make this a real engagement for our whole community. I'd like to find a way to get our students involved, our parents involved, and our faculty and staff. This is a chance for North to get to know some of the folks in the neighborhood and work on making the community better for everybody."

"Glad I stopped you on your way to dinner," Ms. Anderson said. "You've got a deal!"

RESOURCES

Redding, Sam, Marilyn Murphy, and Pam Sheley, eds. *Handbook on Family and Community Engagement*. Lincoln, IL: Academic Development Institute/Center on Innovation & Improvement, 2011.

Winthrop, Rebecca. The Need for Civic Education in 21st-Century Schools. *The Brookings Institution*, June 2020.

8   Co-Teaching

Two or more educators working together to support a common group of students

With policies like the Every Student Succeeds Act (ESSA) and Individuals with Disabilities Education Act (IDEA), schools are faced with the challenge of supporting an increasingly diverse set of learners in an inclusive setting. By taking shared responsibility for the success of their classes, the co-teaching model is meant to provide students with the necessary support to succeed.

Co-teaching (or cooperative teaching) provides teachers an opportunity to collaborate to benefit students who have different learning needs. Two educators working together allows for a smaller teacher-student ratio and thus more individualized student attention for students who may need extra support. It can also reduce the stigma for students who require special support, as they can remain in the classroom rather than leaving to obtain that support separately. Unfortunately, many educators have had no experience or training to execute the strategy effectively.

The most common co-teaching model is, by far, one teacher and one assistant. It can be easily implemented, as the teacher who has developed the lesson for that class period can teach while the co-teacher "assists" as needed. However, a major pitfall for this model is that it often creates an "assistant teacher, head teacher" dynamic in the classroom, and students do not benefit from both teachers' specialized teaching skills. Administrators should be explicit about collaborative co-teaching expectations and provide teachers with adequate common planning time so they can design lessons together rather than separately.

Other co-teaching models, when used strategically to individualize instruction, allow teachers to specifically target groups of students who need extra support or acceleration. However, to be effective, these models require teachers to regularly assess their students. School leaders can support teachers in the use of these models by ensuring teachers are consistently assessing their students, using the data to purposefully group their students, and regularly adapting their instructional methods accordingly.

Team teaching is another co-teaching model that encourages teachers to collaborate with each other to deliver the strongest and most creative lessons. Of all of the co-teaching models, team teaching requires the most experience and planning time to implement. However, it has a myriad of benefits and is the model that can have the most impact when done well. Expert team teaching can truly capitalize on teachers' instructional specialization but requires a tremendous amount of preparation and relationship building for the duo to work seamlessly together in the classroom. Leaders must thoughtfully consider the pairs they establish to bring together teachers who are open to building positive partnerships with a colleague. They must also provide the team teachers ample common planning time to collaboratively plan their lessons.

See also   Differentiation

RESOURCES

Cook, Lynne, and Marilyn Friend. "Co-Teaching: Guidelines for Creating Effective Practices." *Focus on Exceptional Children* 28, no. 3 (January 1995). http://dx.doi.org/10.17161/fec.v28i3.6852.

DOI: 10.4324/9780429321641-8

CASE STUDY

North High's English as a second language (ESL) program was robust. The school board had allowed Jim Short the resources to have two experienced instructors in every ESL classroom. This year, the program had expanded, and Short had staffed it with two new hires, who had a total of ten years' experience teaching ESL.

Nevertheless, when Short visited the new hires in their classroom, he was troubled by what he found. One teacher was teaching the whole class of eighteen students. The other was busily correcting papers. As Short sat in the back of the classroom, the second instructor finished working with the papers and appeared to be preparing a lesson.

Short left them a note asking them to visit him in his office after school.

When they arrived, Short raised his concern.

"When I visited your class today, I saw Annette teaching a very good lesson, but Jeff, you were doing paperwork?"

"That's right. I was grading papers."

"Has either of you ever team taught before?"

Both shook their heads.

Short nodded. "The reason we have two of you in one classroom is to give the kids more contact with teachers. We've found that the more direct contact the kids have with their instructors, the faster they pick up their second language."

"We've been alternating," Annette replied.

"That's what I thought," said Short. "Let me suggest some other strategies. Having two instructors gives you the chance to use a variety of techniques. For example, while Annette is teaching the class, Jeff can roam about and help kids individually.

"It's not uncommon, when you do that," Short continued, "that you'll find several kids are having the same problem. Then you can divide the class up. Annette can continue with the main lesson, and Jeff, you can pull together the kids who need some additional help and work with them.

"And down the road, you might consider really team teaching a lesson. Divide it up and share it, bouncing instruction back and forth. The kids often like that, and it gives you a chance to really understand each other's style."

"That sounds very difficult," Annette said.

"It is," Short replied. "I wouldn't try it until you've worked together for a good while. But it's effective, and you both have had enough experience as teachers that you'd enjoy it."

Cook, Lynne, and Marilyn Friend. *Interactions: Collaboration Skills for School Professionals*, 7th ed. London, England: Pearson, 2013.

9 Crisis Leadership
What you do when the crisis playbook doesn't work

Most schools are proactive about creating crisis plans. Unforeseen events, like natural disasters and inclement weather, warrant clear processes to keep students and faculty safe. However, some crises require leaders to adeptly navigate situations the school may be unprepared to handle. Successful navigation through these rare cases requires the school leader to:

1. Exhibit strong personal leadership
2. Regularly communicate to stakeholders
3. Empower the crisis team to be nimble problem-solvers

A school leader is the face of the organization and thus is uniquely positioned to provide the community with a sense of calm in the midst of a crisis. A crisis requires a school leader who conveys competence, can engender trust, and promotes a clear path forward for the organization. A school leader is always expected to understand their school and community landscape, but this takes on critical importance in responding to a crisis. Leaders should have a nuanced understanding of their school's culture and the surrounding political climate. They need to know their constituencies well—families, students, faculty, and the neighborhood—as well as neighboring schools. During a crisis, these stakeholders will require varying degrees of attention and may be able to provide valuable support.

The leader must prioritize communicating effectively and regularly with stakeholders and avoid being consumed by the details of the crisis. Students, faculty, and families expect to hear from the school leader and will rely on this person to provide updates on how the crisis is progressing. While communication to the media and the public at large may sometimes be tasked to a media or communications director, the school stakeholders will expect the school leader to provide regular communication to them and to provide timely updates, communicate empathy, and articulate a path forward.

The leader's role on the crisis management team should not be to dictate the solution but rather to ensure the team works collaboratively and follows a disciplined, learning-oriented process. It should be clear that the team's goal is not to arrive at some elusive right answer but to work together to solve a unique and complex problem. It may be helpful to assign someone to take an opposing viewpoint as the team iterates on potential solutions. A devil's advocate can be invaluable, as they can uncover blind spots and prevent the team from overinvesting in a convenient solution that may have significant flaws. The team's efforts must also include creating a communication plan for stakeholders and maintaining positive and cooperative relationships with relevant outsiders, such as law enforcement or health officials, depending on the crisis.

See also   Crisis Management, School Climate

RESOURCES

Edmondson, Amy, and Dutch Leonard. "Crisis Management for Leaders: Structuring the Organizational Response." *Webinar from Harvard Business School*, Cambridge, MA, April 10, 2020. www.alumni.hbs.edu/Documents/events/Structuring_the_Organizational_Response_LEONARD%20SLIDE%20PRESENTATION.pdf.

DOI: 10.4324/9780429321641-9

CASE STUDY

The hurricane had been forecast for more than a week, but when the rain and wind hit, the storm was much stronger than anticipated. School was closed, and Jim Short monitored the progress of the storm on his battery-powered radio.

The following day, Short was up at dawn, weaving his way through downed trees and power lines to assess the damage to North High. It was worse than he had feared; the parking lot was flooded, and a large section of the roof over the gym had blown off.

Short found his supervisor of buildings and grounds and got a quick assessment of the damage. Most of the classrooms were intact, but the gym and the lunchroom roofs had been breached, power was out, and there was water in the mechanical room. It was going to take quite a while to regain use of the gym and lunchroom.

Short left campus and drove until he could get a signal on his cell phone. He called the superintendent, who told him the governor was closing schools for the rest of the week. Then he called the leader of his crisis response team (CRT) and told him to initiate the telephone tree and assemble as many members of the CRT as could come. "Bring your notebook," Short said. They had rehearsed a crisis like this just six months ago and had a checklist of what to do.

In just the time he was on the phone, Short noticed his voicemail box was filling up with incoming calls. "Parents," he thought. "They want to know what's happening." He didn't try to return the calls. That was a job for a couple of members of the CRT when they could get a stable phone connection. He rushed back to campus.

As he pulled into the parking lot, he noticed a van from the local TV station setting up its antenna. "Give me a break!" thought Short, but as he walked toward the van, he met the reporter with his friendliest smile. "The school isn't as badly hit as I expected," he said before the reporter could open his mouth.

Short knew his role now was to tell the parents and students of North High what to expect: while cleaning up would be inconvenient, school would go on. The students might be playing their basketball games away this year, and bag lunches were definitely in the forecast. As he answered the reporter's questions about damage to the school, he saw the leader of the CRT drive into the parking lot and start pulling a portable generator out of his trunk. He smiled; that *wasn't* on the list.

Pearson, Christine M., and Judith A. Clair. "Reframing Crisis Management." *Academy of Management Review* 23, no. 1 (January 1998): 59–76. www.jstor.org/stable/259099.

10 Crisis Management

Writing, practicing, and following a crisis playbook

Crises may be rare, but the leader who is unprepared risks the school failing to survive the crisis. A crisis requires swift, decisive action. To manage a crisis, leaders must be directive about process but not about the solution. There are three steps to good crisis management:

1. Prepare
2. Plan
3. Execute

Understanding the landscape of the school and its community is critically important to being prepared for a crisis. Without an understanding of the school culture or local political climate, it is difficult to manage a crisis situation. Crises often arise in response to school policies that are ill-conceived or incomplete. The school leader should identify and build a relationship with the school's legal advisor, as this individual will likely be an important player in managing the crisis. Clear communication with the school's media liaison will prevent mixed messaging and minimize communication gaffes occurring during the crisis.

School leaders should create plans for any crises that can be anticipated. A school evacuation plan and fire safety protocols are common crisis plans every school should have. Assembling a crisis management team is also crucial. This could be the school leadership team, augmented as needed with medical, counseling, and legal experts. The crisis management team's purpose should be to resume normal operations as quickly as possible after a crisis occurs. The crisis management team may need to be modified to add or subtract team members as the nature of the crisis dictates.

A major crisis calls for strong leadership. Leaders should be prepared to act quickly and empower their team to create a path forward. Proactive planning is crucial; during a crisis, it is challenging to think clearly. The school community should be well briefed on the school's crisis plans and should practice regularly so they can be implemented quickly and effectively. But no plan can foresee everything that may occur. Accordingly, swift and well-conceived execution is ultimately most important. The leader must lead in these situations from the front of the crisis and not delegate communication about response or progress to any colleagues.

See also   Crisis Leadership, School Climate, Safety and Security

RESOURCES

Edmondson, Amy, and Dutch Leonard. "Crisis Management for Leaders: Structuring the Organizational Response." *Webinar from Harvard Business School*, Cambridge, MA, April 10, 2020. www.alumni.hbs.edu/Documents/events/Structuring_the_Organizational_Response_LEONARD%20SLIDE%20PRESENTATION.pdf.

Pearson, Christine M., and Judith A. Clair. "Reframing Crisis Management." *Academy of Management Review* 23, no. 1 (January 1998): 59–76. www.jstor.org/stable/259099.

DOI: 10.4324/9780429321641-10

CASE STUDY

One of the first inquiries Jim Short made when he came to North High was whether there was a protocol for how the administration would deal with an unforeseen crisis. His secretary, who had served the two previous principals, responded in three words, "We wing it!"

Short knew that was a mistake and put "crisis management" on a long and growing list of things that needed to be completed yesterday.

Short knew he needed a team that could take on all the operational decisions while they were managing a crisis. While his role as principal was to convene that group and make directional policy decisions, all the details of a crisis—ensuring student and employee safety, managing communications with parents and the press, addressing legal issues—needed to be coordinated by a team able to act without him. He knew that in a crisis, he was going to be tied up at the heart of the action.

Short appointed his senior assistant principal as director of the crisis response team (CRT). Together, they chose members who represented the functional areas likely to be involved in any major crisis. Members included representatives of facilities, security, the school nurse, counseling, and the division heads. Some members were part of the district staff, and Short secured the cooperation of the superintendent. From the district office came representatives of legal affairs, transportation, and media relations.

Short charged this group with coming up with detailed plans for how they would deal with a variety of crises. The list was a long one, and the group was to meet monthly. The CRT identified a conference room near the main office to use as a command center and understood that in the event of a crisis, everyone would congregate in that space.

As the CRT began to come together as a working group, Short directed their attention to understanding the nature of the community they served. Lots of their parents were professionals and would watch the school's efforts to deal with a crisis supportively but would also be quick to be critical if the CRT were clumsy. The CRT needed to get it exactly right.

After six months, they had made great progress, both as a working group and in their crisis planning. It was time for Short to test how well they were doing. Working with a friend at a local college, he found a case study of an explosion in a small chemical plant that had threatened the students and faculty of a nearby school. There was enough data on what had happened to allow him to tell the CRT, "Pretend this happened down the street from us. What would we do?"

11 Curriculum Leadership
Coordinating curriculum design, mapping, and implementation

All well designed curricula reflect three strands that must work together: the intended curriculum, the enacted curriculum, and the assessed curriculum. The intended curriculum contains the learning goals for students and what the faculty use to build their unit and lesson plans. The enacted curriculum encompasses the instructional methods teachers use to teach the intended curriculum to their students. The assessed curriculum is what is measured—either formatively or summatively—and is used to determine if the students are learning the intended content.

School leaders should make sure teachers understand the school's intended curriculum. The intended curriculum is usually adopted from an outside source. Common Core and the International Baccalaureate (IB) Programme are typical intended curricula adopted by many schools. Once the intended curriculum is identified, school leaders must provide time and guidance to fully understand the learning outcomes they need to achieve.

Once teachers have a solid understanding of the school's intended curriculum, they are equipped to design the enacted curriculum. School leaders consistently underestimate the amount of time and preparation needed to plan an enacted curriculum. Both new and veteran teachers should have ample time before school begins to do curriculum planning. Veteran teachers should also be required to share their curriculum documents with first-year teachers, as new teachers will need the most support to create their enacted curriculum maps. Before the first day of school, department heads should review yearly curriculum maps and be sure all teachers have detailed first-unit plans. Throughout the year, leaders should provide teachers with weekly subject and grade team time to vertically and horizontally align their units to the intended curriculum. Monthly professional-development checkpoints should be scheduled throughout the year so teachers can share their enacted curriculum documents with each other. Furthermore, the administration should be consistently providing instructional support to all teachers who need assistance with their curriculum planning.

Finally, school leaders must establish how to assess the enacted curriculum. The assessed curriculum is jointly created by teachers but also often mandated by outside agencies. Many state and city governments require students to take specific exams in order to move to the next grade level. School leaders should encourage teachers to create shorter, more frequent formative and summative assessments that are aligned with their enacted curriculum maps. It is important that these assessments are created collaboratively by grade- and subject-level teams to ensure they are uniformly rigorous and are vertically and horizontally aligned to each other and to the intended curriculum. Leaders can also further reinforce any mandated assessments by having teachers create similar "mock" versions of these exams to provide opportunities for students to demonstrate the enacted curriculum's effectiveness.

See also   Co-Teaching, Instructional Coaching

RESOURCES

Cuban, Larry. "Curriculum Stability and Change." In *Handbook of Research on Curriculum*, edited by Philip Jackson, 246–47. New York: Macmillan, 1992.

DOI: 10.4324/9780429321641-11

CASE STUDY

With the support of the superintendent and a lot of encouragement from Jim Short, the school district decided to implement an International Baccalaureate (IB) track at North High. The IB curriculum and the chance to take the exams for the IB diploma would be available to any student in the district who met the achievement measures the district set.

Short knew the IB curriculum had been in existence for more than fifty years and was precisely written. It was an intended curriculum that had been carefully conceived and revised over time. It was also a curriculum in which the assessments were carefully aligned with the intended curriculum. That placed a lot of responsibility on the shoulders of the faculty to make sure the enacted curriculum really taught the students what they needed to know and to be able to do. He made arrangements for the faculty selected to teach the IB to spend the summer in IB-sponsored training.

Short also had the new IB faculty meet for several days before school began to discuss their plans for enacting the curriculum to which they had been introduced over the summer. While the IB curriculum was well defined and the faculty were aware of the difficult and comprehensive tests students would have to pass to earn the IB diploma, faculty still needed to devise daily lesson plans. Short knew these plans needed to be coordinated, and some faculty, especially relatively inexperienced faculty, would need the help of veteran faculty in bringing the intended curriculum to life.

Finally, Short made sure North High's department chairs met with the IB faculty every two months to discuss alignment issues. While the IB diploma curriculum was a self-contained curriculum, rising tenth-graders needed to be ready to transition to the IB in their eleventh-grade year. Likewise, state-mandated curricular requirements had to be accommodated. Teaching the IB was not as simple as taking a curriculum package and dropping it into North High's program. A great deal of both horizontal and vertical alignment needed to be worked out before the IB program could be successful.

Short had decided the final IB exams would provide the standard for evaluating the effectiveness of the implementation. In consultation with the department chairs and the superintendent, he set a goal of a 90% passing rate to indicate success for the program's first class.

Porter, Andrew C., and John L. Smithson. *Defining, Developing, and Using Curriculum Indicators*. CPRE Research Report Series RR-048, December 2001. Philadelphia, PA: Consortium for Policy Research in Education, University of Pennsylvania Graduate School of Education. www.cpre.org/sites/default/files/researchreport/788_rr48.pdf.

12   Data-Driven Decision-Making
Systematically using data to make informed decisions

Using data in schools is nothing new—test scores and attendance are often metrics that schools use to assess how students are doing. However, using data systematically and comprehensively is where many schools fall short. Data-driven decision-making in education is a process of creating a structure and system to use data to assess how well the school is performing. This process allows the school to use information to identify strategic goals and set yearly priorities. It focuses on using data comprehensively to drive systematic schoolwide progress rather than using data in an ad hoc way. Leaders should support their faculty in utilizing data by:

1. Creating a schoolwide process for data collection and consideration
2. Aligning instructional goals to data metrics
3. Providing regular professional development (PD) time for faculty to analyze and share data

The first step is to identify and collect data that supports wise decision-making around the school's strategic goals. For example, if annual standardized test data indicates that seventh-grade students are reading below grade level, a school could decide to collect monthly reading comprehension assessment grades to see how students are progressing throughout the year. A different example would be collecting student attendance data as an "early-warning indicator" to determine which students are most at risk of going "off track." It is important to keep the data collection process focused on key goals rather than to collect every data point.

Annual instructional goals establish the focus for the year, but for a school to have a true data-driven culture, goals should cascade down from the yearly school goals to grade-level, subject-area teams and to individual teachers themselves. A collaborative approach to data promotes a sense of shared responsibility among teachers.

The school schedule must include time to review and reflect on the salient student and school data. These data reviews should focus on ongoing, interim progress as well as including regular, periodic assessments of progress toward annual goals. Administrators and teachers should analyze standardized test scores, attendance data, and behavior data to make timely decisions for their schools. Creating regular PD cycles in which data can be analyzed by the entire faculty can flag the students who are not performing at grade level and better align the curriculum across departments and grades. Having a regular data cycle structure creates a calendar—and, more importantly, a culture—for how and when the instructional leadership team meets to review ongoing progress. Similarly, it creates a schedule for grade-level and disciplinary teams to meet to discuss progress. Having timely intervals for data analysis allows all teachers to be aware of which students need support so they can leverage shared strategies to support these at-risk learners.

See also   Assessment, Goal Setting, School Climate

RESOURCES

Schmoker, Mike. "Measuring What Matters." *Educational Leadership* 66, no. 4 (December 2008): 70–74. www.ascd.org/el/articles/measuring-what-matters.

DOI: 10.4324/9780429321641-12

CASE STUDY

During his first year at North High, Jim Short attended a conference run by the state principals' association. One of the speakers was the president of the state university, an institution of some 40,000 students, which dominated the life of the small city in which it was located. Short didn't have any expectations for the president's speech, but one story caught his interest.

"We try to measure as many things as we can that impact the experience of our students," the president said. "For example, we keep track of car theft in the surrounding community. You might not think that was relevant to a college education, but we've found that the rise and fall of car theft in our neighborhood directly correlates with the rate of theft and burglary on campus. And that does affect a student's experience."

After the talk, Short made a point of introducing himself to the president. "Could I talk to the person in charge of your institutional research?" he asked.

"Certainly," replied the president. "And I'll have my assistant send you a copy of our annual data report."

Within a few days, Short had the report and had read it thoroughly. He showed it to Mary Kelley, assistant principal, and Dave Gleason, director of operations. "We need to start work on something like this," Short told them. "The university obviously has more staff to collect and analyze data, but they're doing something we're not doing well. They are using data to trigger actions and interventions. Just as an example, they get a monthly statistic from their local police on the number of car thefts and break-ins in their neighborhood. If that rate starts going up, they add security patrols on campus. We don't need that kind of data, but wouldn't it be great if we could collect data early enough in the school year so it would alert teachers which students were headed for trouble with the state exams?"

"You want to set up a system in which we gather data to trigger corrective action?" asked Mary Kelley.

"Exactly," said Short. "I bet a lot of teachers do it already on their own, but it would be helpful if we could look at that data on a schoolwide basis."

"And that would help teachers who were either too new or inexperienced to think of doing it on their own," added Dave Gleason.

"It would also help department chairs who are assessing their curriculum. It would help me in talking to the superintendent. Gosh, it would help me in talking to parents and the faculty in general!" Short replied.

13   Death and Bereavement
Managing loss in a school community

Dealing with the emotional reactions of children, staff, and parents to death and bereavement is far more common than many new school administrators anticipate. School administrators should prepare for the inevitable trauma of death in the community by having four procedures in place:

1. A well-trained crisis response team
2. A communications plan that includes telling faculty, students, and parents of the loss, as well as managing press inquiries
3. Policy on memorials—both planned and spontaneous
4. Plans for the support of grieving members of the community—both short and long term

When the school is notified of the loss of a student or faculty or staff member, the crisis response team should be assembled. It is important for that group to verify—to the extent possible—the details of the fatality. In the case of a student death, the family must be contacted to offer support and sympathy and to determine what information the family would like to have disclosed.

Deaths in a school community are often treated as major news stories. The public information officer should be able to refer to previously designed policies to cover press conferences and the degree to which the press will be allowed to speak to students and faculty. Faculty and relevant staff should be informed first, with students soon after. Those students likely to be very disturbed by the loss should be told in person by faculty, administrators, or counselors who are well known to them.

Memorials will often spontaneously appear at the loss of a student or faculty member. The school should have a policy regarding when memorials will be removed and what will happen to these treasured objects. (They are often given to the family that has lost a loved one.) It is important these policies are uniformly followed; otherwise, grieving families will feel some deaths are being treated as special. In the case of suicide, many schools seek to minimize memorials, since there is some evidence they may encourage other individuals who are considering taking their own lives.

School communities are a good place to provide ongoing support to grieving students and parents. Faculty should be trained to identify the signs that students need help in managing their grief. Schools should be prepared for grief to recur long after the actual death. Anniversaries are always difficult; and in the case of a student death, classmates who shared an activity—a sports team, for example—may encounter situations that bring back troubling feelings for years.

See also   Crisis Management

RESOURCES

National Center for School Crisis and Bereavement. *Guidelines for Responding to the Death of a Student or School Staff*. Los Angeles, CA: National Center for School Crisis and Bereavement, Los Angeles Children's Hospital, August 2020. www.schoolcrisiscenter.org/wp-content/uploads/2020/08/Guidelines-Death-Student-or-Staff-Booklet-Format.pdf.

DOI: 10.4324/9780429321641-13

CASE STUDY

Jim Short had arrived at his office early that morning with the intent of catching up on paperwork before school started. He had just sat down at his desk when his phone began to ring. "Early call," he thought as he answered the phone.

He heard a man sobbing on the other end of the line and saying, over and over, "He's gone. He's gone . . ."

Calling up all his counseling instincts and fueled with a powerful jolt of adrenaline, Short patiently helped the father collect himself and learned what he had feared: that a senior boy, one of the basketball captains, had taken his own life.

Short knew the family and felt he should be the one to be with them at this terrible moment. He also wanted to learn as much as he could of the details of what had happened and what information the family would be willing to make public. That was a lot to ask of a family caught in traumatic grief, but Short knew that if he were to provide support, the family would eventually trust him to help them deal with the public.

"Can I come over to your house?" Short asked.

There was a pause. "Yes," said the father. "The police are still here."

Before he left to be with the family, Short called his assistant principal, Mary Kelley. "Mary," he said, "Terrible news. We've had a student suicide. You know him: Luke, one of the captains of the basketball team." He heard her voice choke. "Sorry to be so brusque, but I'm headed to their house. Could you convene the crisis team—use my office—and notify the superintendent? Also ask the district public information office to join the crisis team. The press is going to go nuts over this. There was an article on the sports page last week wondering what college Luke was going to sign with.

"I know the crisis team is well aware of this," Short said, "but I worry a lot about the potential for a copycat problem in this case. Ask the team to be especially careful about our plan for telling the students. They'll be shocked, and they're going to want to have a massive memorial service. He was a hero to a lot of kids. I worry that the celebration of Luke's life could help push some other kid over the edge."

"I hear you," Mary said.

"I'll check in as soon as I can," said Short. He sprinted for his car, knowing it was going to be weeks before he caught up on his mail.

14 Developmental Coaching

Supporting faculty through the lens of adult development

Developmental coaching differentiates support to individuals depending on where they are in their arc of professional development. It is grounded in the theory that adults have different ways of understanding and experiencing the world and progressing, optimally, on a continuum to ever-higher stages of complexity. According to developmental theory, adults gain an independent sense of self and maturity by reflecting on their life experiences and social interactions. Through developmental coaching, a person can become more in control of their behavior and better able to manage the interpersonal factors that affect them.

School leaders should use developmental coaching to provide appropriate learning opportunities and support to their faculty. It allows leaders to look beneath the surface to identify the underlying motivations of the people in their charge. Developmental coaching helps put challenging behaviors in context and can help a leader better understand a person's actions, leading to a more effective leadership response.

Developmental coaching is distinctive by focusing on a person's efficacy rather than the skill or content to be acquired. It is relational in nature and requires both the coach and the person being coached to establish trust. With developmental coaching, the chronological age of a person does not necessarily correlate to someone's level of maturity. Developmental age correlates to a spectrum that takes into account the habits and routines of an individual throughout the context of their history.

An effective developmental coach identifies the stage of development occupied by the person to be coached. Through understanding where they fall on the continuum, a developmental coach can predict why the person is behaving as they currently are and the underlying motivations for their actions. For instance, if a teacher is frustrated because they feel there are no concrete rules around classroom management in the school, this could be remedied by providing them with consistent norms and practices that they can follow.

As helpful as understanding where someone is on the adult development continuum can be, developmental coaching shouldn't stop there. The job of a developmental coach is also to support them in understanding where they are and how to progress. This can be done through coaching the person in times of stress to question what their motivations are and how this may be impacting their decision-making processes. For example, if a faculty member was having difficulty providing a colleague with adjusting feedback for fear of hurting that person's feelings, the coach could work to help this person understand the importance of providing honest feedback despite the risk of hurt feelings, as ultimately, the purpose of the feedback is to ensure students get the best possible experience in the classroom.

See also   In-the-Moment Feedback, Instructional Coaching, One-on-One Meeting

RESOURCES

Kegan, Robert, and Lisa Laskow Lahey. "From Subject to Object: A Constructive-Developmental Approach to Reflective Practice." Chap. 22 in *Handbook of Reflection and Reflective Inquiry: Mapping a Way of Knowing for Professional Reflective Inquiry*, edited by Nona Lyons. New York: Springer, 2010. https://archive.org/details/handbookreflecti00lyon/page/n466.

DOI: 10.4324/9780429321641-14

CASE STUDY

Keith Burns had been the chair of the science department at North High for three years. Burns had asked for an appointment with Jim Short to discuss a teacher in the department.

"What's up, Keith?" Short asked when Burns entered his office.

"I need some help with Ethan Brown," Burns replied. "He's a very good teacher. He's hardworking, very independent, and creative—all good things. He's designed some chemistry labs that are really special. In fact, I've suggested to him that he should write up a few of his labs and see if he can get a publisher interested. He's that good."

"I'm not seeing a problem yet, Keith," Short laughed.

"The problem is that when someone gives Ethan a suggestion, he ignores it. He seems arrogant. He's one of those people you describe as having a 'self-authoring mind,' and I think it's hurting departmental morale."

"Give me an example."

"He and Jennifer Robbins, the physics teacher, were working on a lab for the advanced chemistry section. Jennifer volunteered. She didn't have to do this."

"What happened?"

"She gave Keith three good ideas for his problem set. She'd worked them all out and documented everything. He rejected them without considering them. She was in tears. I was mad when I heard about it. Ethan and I are meeting tomorrow. How do I make him understand he just can't dismiss his colleagues like that?"

Short thought for a minute. "It's not unusual for people who are very creative and independent to have trouble incorporating other people's ideas into their own work. They're the sort of people who are used to going on their own."

"So what do I say to him?"

"Bring Jennifer's problems to the meeting. Go over them with him and ask him to tell you exactly what he found lacking in them. My guess is he'll admit they are pretty good but he just liked his problems better. Follow up on that. Why does he like his better? It may take a while, but I bet you can get him to see that adding some of Jennifer's work would be good for the problem set, and it certainly would be good for his relationship with his colleagues.

"And then you need to meet with Jennifer. She needs to know you value her work."

15 Differentiation
Adapting and adjusting instruction to meet the learning needs of students

A "one-size-fits-all" approach is inadequate to meet the needs of mixed-ability classrooms— those with students who speak multiple languages or have special needs that require varied instructional strategies. Differentiated instruction allows teachers to vary the pace of their lessons, the task complexity, the modality by which groups of students are learning, and the level of support they provide. School leaders should support faculty in differentiating instruction by:

1. Adopting a clear intended curriculum
2. Providing instructional coaching support
3. Scheduling adequate common planning time

Teachers need a complete understanding of the school's intended curriculum to plan instruction. The intended curriculum is the framework from which the enacted curriculum is built, and it should have clear learning objectives. By utilizing the learning objectives as benchmarks for instruction, teachers can gauge students' content knowledge and conceptual understandings. Without a clear intended curriculum, teachers are unable to create lesson plans or a horizontally and vertically aligned curriculum for the school. Having a clear intended curriculum from which to plan is even more critical when differentiating instruction.

To properly differentiate instruction, teachers must first assess where their students are against intended learning objectives and use this data to understand if the students exceed or fall short in their comprehension of the material. Students who have a firm grasp of the material can be given more challenging tasks or accelerated through more content, while students who struggle can be given extra time or support to aid their mastery of the learning outcomes. Leaders should ensure instructional coaches are available who can support teachers in creating useful assessments and reviewing data for differentiation. Finally, leaders can connect novice teachers who have little experience with differentiation with more seasoned teachers who have provided effective differentiated lessons in the past for students of varying abilities. These instructional coaches should also assist teachers in modifying their lesson plans to accommodate a diverse range of learners.

School leaders must support teachers in differentiating instruction by ensuring common planning time is built into their schedules. Differentiated instruction is complex and requires time to prepare. Having ample time to analyze data, plan lessons, and modify instruction is critical to the process. Moreover, leaders should provide common planning time to teachers who co-teach in the same classroom. Teachers who have the same students in different subject areas also need time to meet with their colleagues to share insights on the differentiation strategies that are working best for them.

See also Co-Teaching, Curriculum Leadership, Instructional Coaching

RESOURCES

Tomlinson, Carol A. *How to Differentiate Instruction in Mixed-Ability Classrooms*, 3rd ed. Alexandria, VA: Association for Supervision and Curriculum Development, 1995.

DOI: 10.4324/9780429321641-15

CASE STUDY

While North High had a reasonably stable enrollment, families were always coming and going. Parents found new jobs and moved away, while new families moved into the neighborhood, because North was a well-regarded school with a reputation for strong academic performance. Inevitably, each year, there were new students, many joining in the middle of the academic year, who didn't come equipped with the background they would have had if they had begun North as ninth graders. And inevitably as well, there were continuing students who had learning differences that made some of their required subjects challenging.

Jim Short brought this subject up regularly in meetings with his department chairs. "Teachers need to be able to differentiate their lesson plans," Short said. "Not every student learns the same way; and some, who may have high aptitude, just haven't been exposed to the material we expect our kids to master."

The problem of differentiation tended to be most acute in those courses that assumed a highly sequential development of fundamental skills—especially languages and math. Short had developed a network of instructional coaches to work with faculty in every department, but he allocated extra coaching time to his math and language faculty to accommodate this need. Often, the difficulty that faced teachers in differentiating their instruction was figuring out where the gaps were in a student's background. Students instinctively compensated when they confronted material they didn't understand, and that compensation often obscured the fundamental lack of preparation that caused the problem. Instructional coaches could help faculty sort out these complex cases.

At the heart of the problem of assessing where a student needed additional support was the intended curriculum. Short remembered his early days of teaching, when the "curriculum" was simply a reading list or, often, just a textbook to be completed by the end of the academic year. North High's current curriculum defined clearly the specific skills and content areas the students needed to master. Faculty and instructional coaches trying to discover where a student needed extra help had clear benchmarks to guide their investigation.

Such an investigation, however, took time. And before Short had tweaked the North High schedule to give faculty ample planning time, just finding the time to plan differentiated instruction was hard to come by. In addition to meeting with instructional coaches, faculty often needed to meet colleagues from other academic areas to coordinate plans. A learning challenge that affected a student in language class might also affect the student in history, science, or any subject that required significant reading. Coordination was key. And student success, Short believed, was often the result of careful differentiation at a key moment.

Wormeli, Rick. *Differentiation: From Planning to Practice Grades 6–12*. Portsmouth, NH: Stenhouse Publishers, 2007.

16 Discipline

Expectations and consequences for student behavior

School discipline articulates the rules and strategies to support students in managing their behavior. It should never be punitive but rather should emphasize prevention and intervention strategies to improve behaviors. School leaders should create a code of conduct as well as adopt a discipline policy—two very different tools that should be used in tandem to set guidelines for student behavior.

A school's discipline code explains the standards of behavior set forth by the school. Besides articulating the rules, discipline codes should also explain the responses and consequences for misbehavior. Typically, school discipline codes are adopted from a central or district office but should be created by the school if there is no larger entity that supports the school. All school discipline codes should also articulate the behavioral interventions that support students who may violate the code. While every discipline code should have consequences for violations, it should not be presented as a strictly punitive system. The document should describe a cascade of interventions and supports that encourage prevention and self-regulation.

School leadership should track the number and type of infractions that occur on campus, as well as collecting data on the discipline outcomes for different student groups (i.e., by gender, race, or age). Analyzing this data will help the school identify any potential disciplinary challenges that will need to be addressed and prevent any systemic bias in how students are treated. Research has found that minority students are disproportionately suspended and expelled, while students with disabilities are twice as likely to receive an out-of-school suspension as their nondisabled peers. With the adoption of a discipline code must come communication and fair enforcement to maintain a positive school climate. Schools that have discipline codes that are not followed and enforced suffer the same poor climate issues as those that have no system at all.

In contrast to the school's discipline policy, a school's code of conduct is broader and includes the positive behaviors the school community agrees to embrace together. For example, a code of conduct might deal with inclusion and diversity, as the intent of the code is to ensure all students and faculty feel safe in the school community. Furthermore, codes of conduct might also include guidelines about academic integrity. The code of conduct can have expectations about classroom respect and civility, hall etiquette, school uniform requirements, and commitment to academic excellence. School codes of conduct are usually crafted by the faculty and student body of the school. This is deliberately done, as creating the code requires the school community to articulate how they believe people should treat each other in school.

See also   Operational Excellence, School Climate

RESOURCES

Bear, George G. *School Discipline and Self-Discipline: A Practical Guide to Promoting Prosocial Student Behavior*. New York, NY: Guilford Press, 2010.

DOI: 10.4324/9780429321641-16

CASE STUDY

When Jim Short became the principal of North High, he made a detailed study of the school discipline code and the statistics about the cases handled under it. In general, Short concluded the discipline system worked well and fairly. There were two classes of infraction in North's discipline system. Routine or minor infractions, such as chronic lateness, parking violations, and inappropriate behavior, were handled by the assistant principal, who made sure the discipline system ran in an orderly fashion. More serious infractions—cheating, stealing, or fighting, for example—were sent to a discipline committee composed of three faculty and two seniors who were elected by the student government. The discipline committee heard the evidence collected by the assistant principal and interviewed the student accused of serious misbehavior. Students were allowed to choose a teacher to accompany them for support and advocacy when they appeared before the discipline committee. Over time, punishments, such as suspension, had become standardized, so most students knew what they might expect if they were, for example, caught cheating on a test.

Short studied carefully the past few years of records of the punishments handed out by the discipline committee. He looked for evidence that particular students—such as athletes—received different sentences from the norm. He looked at gender and race to see if there were concerning patterns. He was pleased to see the records were well maintained and didn't reveal any systemic unfairness in the administration of discipline.

What Short didn't find, however, was anything that encouraged the students to develop positive behaviors. There was no explicit code of conduct, and that bothered him. In discussing this with his senior staff, he said, "Our student handbook focuses entirely on the kinds of behavior that aren't permitted. We need to have a list of good behaviors we want students to do—for example, welcoming strangers, putting good sportsmanship ahead of winning, and being inclusive of all the different students in this school."

Short appointed a committee to help draft a code of conduct for North High. He asked the student government to select students to be on the committee, while he and the president of the parents' committee selected parents. He selected faculty members as well as a member of the facilities staff and one from the dining hall staff. He considered those latter appointments essential, since nonteaching staff often observe student behavior in unsupervised locations.

By the end of the year, North High had a code of conduct that Short considered a positive companion to its discipline system.

Darling-Hammond, Sean, Trevor A. Fronius, Hannah Sutherland, Sarah Guckenburg, Anthony Petrosino, and Nancy Hurley. "Effectiveness of Restorative Justice in US K–12 Schools: A Review of Quantitative Research." *Contemporary School Psychology* 24, no. 3 (May 24, 2020): 295–308. https://doi.org/10.1007/s40688-020-00290-0.

17   Double-Loop Learning

A reflective process that promotes growth and improvement

Many schools explicitly schedule regular time to analyze formative data they've collected and assess progress toward goals, but few engage in a degree of reflection that could include major organizational pivots from chosen strategies early in the school year. Chris Argyris describes this act of reflection after analysis as "double-loop" learning—the modification of goals or strategies in light of experience, the data from classrooms. His classic example is of a thermostat that turns on and off when the room temperature reaches 68 degrees. The thermostat performs this task because it receives information (the temperature of the room) and therefore takes corrective action. However, if the thermostat could question itself about why it should be set at 68 degrees, it would be capable not only of detecting error but of questioning the underlying decision-making that was involved. Many schools take time to analyze data and assess it against goal retainment, but most do not reflect on why that particular data was collected nor on why certain strategies were employed in the first place. To do so pushes school personnel beyond asking how they are doing and instead forces the question of why they are doing it.

For decades, other industries have used looped learning as a method for developing their learning cultures and increasing their efficacy. They understand every moment is a "learning opportunity," whether it is a success, partial success, or even failure. For example, hospitals use "morbidity" studies, the Air Force utilizes "after-action" reviews, and NASA employs technical crew debriefing even when the mission has been successful. Whether interacting with the schoolwide instructional leadership team, grade teams, or individual teachers, a leader's reaction to uneven or failing teacher performance must signal the preeminence of a learning culture. American schools, unlike industries and armed forces, typically respond to failure punitively and with blame instead of seeing failure as an opportunity to learn.

Instead, a leader should encourage groups of teachers to take calculated risks, such as an inquiry cycle in which they test a hypothesis on improving instruction over a short period of time and then assess the evidence. Even if successful, the experiment provides an opportunity for improvement and learning. There are times for accountability; but in a learning culture, despite failures, teachers together have embraced continuously improving their classroom performance no matter how well their students do on state tests or college entrance exams. As a result, the resisters who can't appreciate looped learning or a robust learning culture find the exit door.

See also   Innovation Leadership, Piloting Crazy Ideas

RESOURCES

Argyris, Chris, and Donald A. Schön. *Organizational Learning: A Theory of Action Perspective*. Reading, MA: Addison-Wesley, 1978.

DOI: 10.4324/9780429321641-17

Katherine Thomas was the chair of the English department at North High. In Jim Short's view, she was both highly experienced and energetic. She had made an appointment to speak with him.

"What's up, Katherine?"

"Test scores, Jim. We're having trouble moving our averages on the state exams."

"They're not bad. They could always be higher, but they don't indicate any problem. They're stuck at a pretty good level."

"That's true, Jim. I'd say we're about a B+. But B+ isn't the most satisfying grade. The department has been talking about this for over a year, and there's some frustration that we can't get our kids to the A level."

"I can understand that," Jim replied. "What can I do to help?"

"We're having a department meeting next week devoted to this topic. Could you come?"

"Of course."

Shortly after their meeting, Katherine sent Jim a series of planning memos the English department had circulated internally over the previous year. Jim read them carefully and saw the department had been working hard on coming up with a strategy to raise test scores.

When he got to the meeting, he started with what he had read.

"Katherine sent me a number of your planning memos from last year, and I was very impressed by them. You've been trying hard to see how far you can push the traditional English curriculum we teach here at North and make it more effective. That's really good. I congratulate you all."

"But it isn't working," came a voice from the back of the room.

"Why do you think it's not working?" asked Jim.

"We don't know for sure," said Katherine. "But we think we need to do more composition work, starting in grade nine."

"That seems like an easy change," said Jim. "Can't you just assign more compositions?"

"There's a trade-off, Jim. If we want to do more composition work the right way, it means more time working one-on-one with kids, more time helping them rework papers. It could mean less reading and discussion."

"Ah, I see the problem, Katherine. Let me suggest this. Why don't you plan an experiment and call it that? Pick several classes of kids and give them a curriculum with more composition work. Run the experiment for as long as you need, at least a year, and study the effect. If it works well, you can announce success and change it for everyone. If it doesn't work, you'll know to try something else. But most importantly, don't give up on trying to make the curriculum more effective. That's the big goal."

18 Ethical Misconduct

Illicit activity with the potential to disrupt the school community

In the last twenty years, the popular press and much research literature has focused on the problem of teacher–student sexual harassment in K–12 schools. Such illicit activity requires clear policy, robust professional development, and careful enforcement by school administrators. However, school administrators are also likely to have to discipline faculty and other school employees for lesser—but no more ethical—activities such as petty theft, fraud, and driving under the influence. Union contracts may define how these behaviors—which largely take place out of the school building—are handled. In the absence of union or school board guidelines, school administrators will have to find equitable responses to ethical misconduct by school employees.

Administrators who must deal with instances of ethical misconduct in the absence of specific school board or union procedures that cover these situations will be greatly aided by having the following procedures clearly defined in the employee manual:

1. Policies in place that clearly define what constitutes actionable misconduct by school employees. These policies should have careful legal review to ensure the rights of neither the employee nor the school are violated.
2. A clear definition of the process to be followed when actionable misconduct is reported. It is highly advisable to have the school's or the district's attorney be a part of the investigative process.
3. The capacity to suspend the employee from his or her duties during the investigative process so the employee may prepare a defense and so the school community is not distracted by what is happening.

The creation of language defining what constitutes actionable misconduct and appropriate school reactions when such conduct is reported should not be a creative exercise. Most school attorneys have access to boilerplate statements that have been tested in court. Likewise, neighboring schools and school districts, as well as state and national educational associations, have such language available. As enforcement of rules against misconduct may well carry liability for the school taking action, it is wise to use language that has been carefully reviewed and tested in actual cases.

It is equally important for school administrators to view an employee caught in misconduct with a degree of empathy and an inclination to mercy. Often, these cases result from employees struggling with emotional issues, drug addiction, or marital discord. Counseling and mental health care may be as necessary a reaction to the misconduct as a prescribed punishment. A school is a community, and there are lessons to be taught to all members of the community by the way the school and its administrators administer justice.

See also   Termination, Situational Decision-Making, Crisis Management

RESOURCES

Zubay, Bongsoon, and Jonas F. Soltis. *Creating the Ethical School: A Book of Case Studies*. New York: Teachers College Press, 2005.

DOI: 10.4324/9780429321641-18

Ellen Bonds was the head of food services at North High. Jim Short thought she knew her job, kept excellent track of hygiene and regulatory issues, and never failed to make her budget. This morning, he popped his head in her office.

"Good morning, Ms. Bonds. Everything well in food land?"

"Glad you're here, Principal Short. I was coming to see you."

"When you call me Principal Short, I know it's trouble, Ellen. What's up?"

"I think somebody is stealing from the storeroom—and not small quantities. Boxes of canned soup, cooking oil, things like that. I was in the storeroom a couple of weeks ago, and something didn't seem right. It's not time for a full inventory yet, so I took pictures with my cell phone. I checked again yesterday, and sure enough, about ten items, mostly boxes of food, have disappeared. Gone."

Short thought for a moment. The district guidelines required him to report this to law enforcement, but having a cruiser show up and detectives going through the kitchen would cause a huge commotion. It might also trigger union action. The food service workers were all unionized.

"I've got a hunch about a suspect," Ellen continued. "Warren Bunnell. I've bumped into him in the kitchen at odd hours after the kitchen is closed. He said he forgot things and came back after practice to get them. He seemed unusually nervous."

"Ouch," replied Short. Warren Bunnell had a second job as girls' varsity basketball coach. He was immensely popular. "Does he have a key to the storeroom?"

"No, but he knows where the key is kept. He could get in."

"Any idea why he might want to risk stealing?"

"No, although I know his wife got laid off. Maybe they're short of money."

"Or food," Short said. It troubled him to think that Warren Bunnell might be so desperate that he'd risk his job and his public position with the girls' basketball team to steal food. He wished there were a way to unwind this situation and help Warren out with his personal problem before he had risked a greater problem by stealing.

"We don't have a lot of options, Ellen. The district wants us to report suspected theft to the superintendent's office and the police. I'll let the superintendent know and have a talk with the police chief. I'd like to investigate this as sensitively and privately as we can. Regardless of whether or not it's Warren, if it's one of our people, it's going to be a trauma for the school. We can't have stealing, but I hope we don't have to ruin someone's life to stop it."

19 Faculty Evaluation

A summative review of teacher performance

Faculty evaluation is a system by which teachers' performance and effectiveness are reviewed and rated. Such systems commonly take into account how teachers deliver instruction in the classroom, how they contribute to the school culture and community, and their overall impact on student achievement.

Many faculty evaluation systems do not effectively measure teacher quality, primarily due to a failure to establish clear standards. Without clear standards, evaluation systems cannot discriminate between effective and ineffective teachers, so the vast majority of teachers receive satisfactory ratings. The bulk of teacher evaluation systems focus on a single measure: classroom observations conducted by a school administrator. Such systems hinge on one or two yearly observations by an administrator who utilizes professional judgment to rate the teacher. Most teacher evaluations are heavily subjective and poor measures of teacher effectiveness.

However, there are teacher evaluation systems that work. The Gates Foundation's Measures of Effective Teaching (MET), the most comprehensive study of faculty evaluation systems to date, found that the use of multiple measures—including evidence of student achievement gains, observational scores based on multiple classroom observations, and feedback from student surveys—was the most effective way to assess a teacher's impact on student learning. Before the MET study, many school districts believed the most important contributors to teacher effectiveness were factors like years of teacher experience or completion of a graduate degree program. This is not the case.

Five characteristics that distinguish effective faculty evaluation systems:

1. Evaluation tools are simple and focus on just a few high-impact strategies
2. Evaluation rubrics drive classroom observation, goal setting, feedback, and personnel decisions
3. Supervisors coach as well as evaluate teachers
4. Teachers receive feedback from multiple stakeholders and sources
5. Evaluation data inform teacher development, pay, and promotion decisions

An effective evaluation tool should generally have between three and five domains, each with three to five specific indicators (skills or practices). The tool should not have more than twenty-five indicators. Domains should correspond to the essential components of a teacher's professional responsibilities, such as effective teaching practices, evidence of student achievement, high student engagement, and overall contributions to school culture. Domains should also differentiate the teacher's skill level, using a developmental scale with four or five categories, from novice to expert. Supervisors should use evaluation tools to both coach and evaluate teachers.

To be effective, the teacher evaluation system should incorporate regular teacher feedback from multiple sources and stakeholders. Feedback should come in the form of peer observations, one-on-one meetings with a supervisor, student and parent engagement survey data, and monthly formal classroom observations. Finally, teacher evaluation data should govern personnel decisions and directly drive decisions about compensation, promotion, retention, or dismissal.

See also In-the-Moment Feedback, One-on-One Meeting

DOI: 10.4324/9780429321641-19

CASE STUDY

Jim Short always remembered his first experience of being "evaluated" as a beginning teacher. The assistant principal for instruction took a chair in the back of his class and put a clipboard on the desk in front of him. Short concentrated on teaching his lesson. About 15 minutes later, the assistant principal got up and let himself out with a friendly wave. Short could see the clipboard had no writing on it.

Several months later, Short had a meeting with the assistant principal. "You were fine, Jim," the assistant principal said. "No complaints. Good work. Are you coming back next year?"

Even though he was a beginning teacher, Short realized he had missed a chance to improve his teaching.

When Short took over North High, the superintendent told him one of his goals was to improve faculty evaluation systemwide. He told Short there were three main elements to making faculty evaluation successful: considering valid data about student performance, having multiple people perform classroom observation, and using student feedback.

While there was considerable anxiety about changing an evaluation system a lot like the one he had known as a new teacher, Short found faculty who would help him plan a new system to meet the superintendent's goals. He asked his colleagues three questions: What performance data is an accurate measure of student performance? Who should be involved in assessing the teacher in the classroom? And how could student feedback be incorporated into the overall assessment?

It took about a year to reach consensus on a new faculty evaluation plan for North High. Short and his colleagues defined several critical testing measures to index student performance. They agreed every faculty member being evaluated would get multiple classroom visits from at least three different people, including peers. They also agreed the evaluators could not leave with a blank clipboard but had to follow each visit with a session that was *both* evaluation and coaching. Student feedback was collected through an anonymous questionnaire whose questions were public and reflected the review and input of faculty. Finally, each review cycle ended with the teacher, Short, and his assistant principal meeting to establish goals and frankly discussing the impact of the review on salary and promotion.

RESOURCES

Darling-Hammond, Linda, Audrey Amrein-Beardsley, Edward Haertel, and Jesse Rothstein. "Evaluating Teacher Evaluation." *Phi Delta Kappan* 93, no. 6 (March 2012): 8–15. https://doi.org/10.1177 %2F003172171209300603.

Bill & Melinda Gates Foundation. *Learning About Teaching: Initial Findings from the Measures of Effective Teaching Project*. Seattle, WA, 2012. https://docs.gatesfoundation.org/documents/preliminary-findings-research-paper.pdf.

White, Taylor. *Evaluating Teachers More Strategically: Using Performance Results to Streamline Evaluation Systems*. Carnegie Foundation for the Advancement of Teaching, January 2014. www.carnegiefoundation. org/wp-content/uploads/2014/12/BRIEF_evaluating_teachers_strategically_Jan2014.pdf.

20 Goal Setting

Articulating what the team seeks to accomplish

Goal setting is a necessary first step to successfully achieving a desired outcome. There are four essential questions to keep in mind when engaging in effective goal setting:

1. Is your goal specific?
2. Is your goal sufficiently difficult?
3. Is your goal public?
4. Is your goal shared?

Specific goals help pinpoint what should be prioritized for increased performance. General instructions to "do your best" or providing no guidance on priorities increase ambiguity around what to do or do next. Clear goals signal multiple opportunities for course correction as strategies are executed—like ship captains repeatedly checking navigation against the North Star. Goal difficulty adds intensity and increases the amount of effort needed to achieve the goal. But difficult goals that are also attainable lead to increased performance. If the goal is too ambitious, the odds of giving up are high. Moreover, public goals increase both personal accountability and the potential for success. When others become aware of a goal, they're more likely to offer suggestions, positive reinforcement, or referrals to helpful resources. Finally, having a shared goal allows for collaboration and social connections. When individuals in an organization have shared goals, they have the opportunity to push each other's performance and can achieve more as a team than they could individually.

Schools have two types of goal setting: organizational goal setting and individual goal setting. Organizational goal setting should be closely aligned to the school's mission and vision. A school's goals are often articulated as a thematic goal—an organizational goal that is time-bound and measurable. School leaders should choose one thematic goal that can be clearly communicated to the rest of the school. The thematic goal should cascade from the leadership team down to the individual level. For instance, if the school's goal is to increase student achievement on a particular standardized test, a cascading goal might be for divisional teams to improve student performance on quarterly grade-level assessments that are aligned to the standardized test. Similarly, smaller grade teams could then create goals that align to the larger divisional goal. An aligned grade team's goal could be to improve student performance on commonly missed question types on a particular exam. Individual goal setting is also important, as it encourages conversations between employees and managers about performance evaluation. When employees are involved in goal setting and participate in choosing their own course of action, they are more likely to fulfill their responsibilities and achieve agreed-upon performance targets.

See also In-the-Moment Feedback, School Climate

RESOURCES

Epton, Tracy, Sinead Currie, and Christopher J. Armitage. "Unique Effects of Setting Goals on Behavior Change: Systematic Review and Meta-Analysis." *Journal of Consulting and Clinical Psychology* 85, no. 12 (December 2017): 1182–98. http://dx.doi.org/10.1037/ccp0000260.

DOI: 10.4324/9780429321641-20

CASE STUDY

"Jim," wrote the math chair, Dick Brown, "the department and I would like to propose an experimental change in the AP calculus curriculum. Traditionally, we've followed the published AP curriculum pretty closely, but recently, we've discovered a curriculum that places a lot more focus on problem-solving and discovery. We think it will be more successful. We'd like to make this an option the kids can choose for the next two years to give us time to track results and see if we want to make a complete shift."

Short was always in favor of faculty being innovative, and he liked that the math department was setting a stretch goal for itself. It would be easy and safe to use the standard AP curriculum, but to try to push beyond it—that was ambitious. He called a meeting with Brown, the calculus teachers, and his senior administrative team.

"Let me start," Short said as the group assembled, "by congratulating you for wanting to take on this kind of challenge. That's good teaching. Let me ask a few questions to frame where I think this experiment should go.

"First, what exactly is the goal? Are you hoping to raise AP scores? We need a clear target.

"Second, is this a big enough experiment? Do you need to make other changes to the tenth- or eleventh-grade curriculums to prepare kids for this senior-level study?

"And third, how public are you going to be in what you're trying to do? There'll be more pressure on you to succeed if you tell people what the long-range goal is, and there'll also be more naysayers trying to talk you out of taking this risk."

"Jim," Dick Brown replied, "I knew you'd have hard questions. But the department has talked a lot about this, and here's what we think. Yes, we'll use AP scores as a measure, but we want to use some internal tests we'll develop, and we want to survey the kids to see their satisfaction and anxiety levels. We plan to introduce a 'math club' approach for eleventh graders thinking of taking this course. It may not be enough, but it's a start. And finally, we're proud of the work we've done on this. Let's tell everybody and see if we can build some positive excitement!"

Locke, Edwin, and Gary P. Latham. *A Theory of Goal Setting and Task Performance*. Englewood Cliffs, NJ: Prentice Hall, 1990.

21 Grading
A system to communicate student learning

Critics of grading point out that grades are invalid, inaccurate, and demoralizing for students and reduce rather than enhance student learning. Grading can be every bit as bad as this, but it doesn't have to be. Grading holds students and schools accountable for learning and simply and unambiguously communicates student achievement. But how do schools maximize the benefit of clear communication to students and families while minimizing the negative impact on student learning?

Schools should ensure their grades:

1. Are based on a system of assessment that authentically measures student learning against published standards. Enough objective information should be used to calculate grades so they are an accurate reflection of student learning.
2. Are simple and clear. Parents and older students should be able to understand the information used to calculate grades and to calculate the grades themselves. While complex methods to calculate grades are available (e.g., Power Law), the system will fail through lack of trust and transparency if the methods are unintelligible.
3. Can be changed. Students should be able to improve their grades to achieve their goals.
4. Include written feedback to motivate students to improve their learning behaviors; provide two or three pieces of advice to meet long-term learning goals.
5. Include both effort and achievement, although given as separate grades.

Several systems of grading are common; all compare students, either to other students (norm-referenced) or to expectations (criterion-referenced). Criterion-referenced systems are preferable, as they focus attention on learning achievement rather than on other students and thus are more understandable, actionable, and motivating to students.

Most school leaders who wade into this controversial topic have battle scars. To establish or reestablish grading policies at the school, follow five steps:

1. Set and socialize the purpose and goals of grading.
2. Make clear the expectations for learning achievement and communicate these expectations through intended standards and learning outcomes.
3. Establish a system of assessment that is accurate and reflects the goals and the learning standards.
4. Design the grading system using the rules above. **Avoid the trap of starting with the fourth step.**
5. Standardize the system across all teachers and grades, and publish it. **Avoid the trap of skipping the fifth step.**

Is it possible to avoid the controversy? Probably not; so implementing a change management strategy along with periodic review and revision of the grading system will be crucial to success.

See also   Curriculum Leadership

DOI: 10.4324/9780429321641-21

CASE STUDY

From the moment he arrived at North High, Jim Short knew he was going to have to do something about the grading system. He didn't look forward to the task. He knew that nothing risked stirring the passion of faculty, students, and their parents more than changes to the grading system. Even if everyone agreed there were problems, a flawed system that was familiar was preferable to an unfamiliar one.

North had a traditional norm-referenced system. If the average grade on a math test was 60%, that became the "C" level, even though it indicated the average student didn't understand 40% of the material. Short believed in a criterion-referenced system, in which achievement levels were defined in advance and student work measured against them.

Short knew that to change the grading system, he would have to convince faculty, parents, and students of the advantages of the new system. He began with the faculty. He contracted with a professor of education at the local university to give his department chairs a workshop on criterion-based grading. Step by step, he introduced the idea to faculty and then to students and parents.

Once some momentum began to build for criterion-based grading, Short asked each department to create a working group to define standards related to the goals of the department's intended curriculum. Again, he needed help from the professor of education, who had become interested in Short's effort to improve the grading system. Once the working groups had defined the learning standards for their disciplines, the department chairs led a long series of departmental conversations to train faculty in how the new system would work.

Once the faculty had begun work on the new standards, Short never missed an opportunity to talk to parents and students about the change they were investigating. Students, of course, were initially the most concerned. Would this mean it was harder to make the honor roll? No, Short replied, and he arranged to have representatives of a school with criterion-based grading give an assembly presentation.

Finally, with the approval of the superintendent, Short was ready to implement the new grading system. It hadn't been easy, and it had taken time. Some people were unhappy. But Short was confident the change was the right one.

RESOURCES

Guskey, Thomas R. *On Your Mark: Challenging the Conventions of Grading and Reporting.* Bloomington, IN: Solution Tree Press, 2014.

Marzano, Robert J. *Formative Assessment and Standards-Based Grading.* Bloomington, IN: Solution Tree Press, 2010.

22 Hiring

A systematic approach to assembling the best-fit team for the school

Hiring the right staff is critical to the success of a school. A school must have three hiring practices in place to successfully hire a quality faculty:

1. Selection model
2. Hiring team
3. Timeline

A selection model enables the school to find the faculty who are the right fit for the school. A school leader should consider the unique qualities of the school program and emphasize them during the selection process. For instance, if the school has a project-based curriculum, the hiring team should ask the candidates directly about their ability and experience to create project-based activities. A solid selection process asks candidates to demonstrate their competency through a demonstration lesson or an on-demand task. In addition to academic and teaching abilities, a prospective candidate should be asked to speak about their personal commitment to education and demonstrate their ability to connect with students. However, creating an arduous series of performative tasks and hour-long interviews is both unfair to the candidate and exhausting for the hiring team, so both should be avoided.

School leaders can be a part of the team or have designated a senior member of the leadership team, who has an experienced instructional background, to manage the hiring process. Leaders should also ask members of the school faculty to assist in the hiring process. School faculty members should only be chosen if they can devote the time to the process and have the requisite disposition and teaching expertise to be helpful in finding the right candidates. The decision to add a faculty member to the team should be deliberate and strategically made. Finally, the hiring committee should be kept small (no more than four to six members) and should remain stable to maintain consistent rating from candidate to candidate.

In a typical school year, the teacher recruitment and hiring season starts in January, with the peak of hiring season in early spring. Schools should complete their hiring process by May, since many of the best prospects have already committed to other schools after this point. The hiring team should attend teacher recruitment fairs and send out job postings and inquiries to graduate schools of education in the fall before the hiring season begins. Once resumes begin to roll in, administrative members of the team should assist in vetting candidates and scheduling interviews and demonstration lessons. The hiring team leader should utilize a shared calendar to organize the days and time for interviews and demos. Using a team and a robust and specific selection model, the hiring process will be time intensive. Leaders should understand that having an organized hiring calendar and devoting the necessary time and resources to hiring are critically important.

See also   Admissions, Leadership Team

RESOURCES

Hughes, Thomas Ross. "Hiring At Risk: Time to Ensure Hiring Really Is the Most Important Thing We Do." *NCPEA International Journal of Educational Leadership Preparation* 9, no. 1 (March 2014).

DOI: 10.4324/9780429321641-22

CASE STUDY

Happily, the faculty at North High was quite stable; but Jim Short knew some turnover was normal and good. Every year after Thanksgiving, he sent a note to all his faculty and senior administrative staff asking them to let him know by February 1 if they were planning on not returning for the coming year. Not everybody would respond to that request. Short knew some faculty were fearful of letting him know they were looking for another job, but a surprising percentage did let him know.

Short wanted to get his hiring process underway as soon after January 1 as possible. He wanted North to be the first school to make an offer to the right candidates. Over the years, Short had found the process worked best if he created a small three- to four-person hiring committee for each open position. As chair, he selected a strong faculty member or administrator with the skill and experience to judge the candidate's academic preparedness and teaching skill. North's HR director held a training session for the hiring committees to make sure they understood the best practices to ensure a fair and inclusive process. Short never sat on the hiring committees himself. He always tried to talk to all candidates twice when they visited the school, briefly at the start of their day to welcome them and for a longer period after their interviews and demonstration teaching, to judge their insight into the culture and educational philosophy of North High.

Scheduling candidates to interview and do teaching demonstrations could be a nightmare. Short assigned a senior HR assistant to handle scheduling for each hiring committee. It was that person's job to make sure interviews were paced so the same classes were not disrupted by candidates' demonstration teaching and the candidates had clear schedules to follow when they arrived on campus. Often, the HR assistant would meet the candidate as they followed their schedule to make sure they could find their way to their next appointment.

Short instructed his hiring committee chairs to obtain letters of recommendation, student testimonials (if available), and any supportive material, such as published articles, from the candidates. He also asked them to have the candidate supply three new references who could be called. Short liked to call the principal of the candidate's school himself as a final step if the hiring committee recommended a candidate. Short met with the hiring committee after they had seen all the finalists and were ready to make a recommendation. Short reserved the final decision on hiring for himself, but he rarely disagreed with a hiring committee.

23 In-the-Moment Feedback

Observing behaviors and offering real-time feedback to improve performance

In-the-moment feedback is essential to adult learning. This type of feedback differs from the comprehensive feedback delivered during performance reviews, as it focuses on behaviors in the moment rather than quarterly or yearly goals or summative performance objectives. Effective supervisors can use it as an instructional coaching tool to impact classroom practice.

Communicating frequently and specifically about observed performance is at the heart of effective in-the-moment feedback. However, most administrators don't have training on how to do this. A few conditions need to be met to ensure the feedback is positively received. First, a supervisor must begin by building a trusting relationship with the teacher. Research on feedback states that trust building usually occurs through weekly or biweekly one-on-one meetings in which the supervisor prioritizes getting to know the teacher's work. Once trust has been established, the supervisor should inform the teacher they will be providing in-the-moment feedback, clearly indicating the in-the-moment feedback will focus on observable behaviors and will be regularly administered. The supervisor should begin by emphasizing affirming feedback and move cautiously toward more adjusting feedback so they do not disrupt the trust that has been established. Current positive psychology research literature indicates that the ideal ratio of praise to critical feedback is 6:1 among the highest-functioning teams in a given organization.

Once these pre-conditions are met, in-the-moment feedback is a three-step process:

1. The supervisor should first ask if they can give in-the-moment feedback. This allows the supervisor to leverage the trusting relationship with the teacher and provides an indication of whether the teacher is in the right mental state to receive the feedback.
2. The supervisor should name the behavior observed and immediately follow with a statement of the outcome that was connected to the behavior. By doing this, the supervisor makes the causality of the behavior clear to the teacher.
3. Finally, the supervisor should affirm the positive behavior or, if adjusting feedback was given, ask for the teacher to make a change.

In-the-moment feedback is only effective when delivered within a 36-hour window. Beyond this time frame, there is a drop-off in understanding, clarity, and effectiveness. If in-the-moment feedback cannot be provided within this time, it should not be given. The prime focus of the in-the-moment feedback process should be to influence the teacher's future performance. Effective feedback always means thinking about the future. Dwelling on past mistakes automatically creates a defensive dynamic. There is nothing the supervisor (or teacher) can do about the past; only future behavior can be improved through timely and actionable in-the-moment feedback.

See also   Instructional Coaching, One-on-One Meeting

DOI: 10.4324/9780429321641-23

CASE STUDY

Jim Short was a firm believer that education always worked best when experienced in context. It was one thing to talk to a teacher about a pedagogical theory, but if you sat in a teacher's class and pointed out when they had done something well or when something needed adjustment, those were the lessons that stuck.

Short tried to encourage his department chairs and assistant principals to spend as much time as possible in classrooms giving immediate, contextual feedback. The first thing, he emphasized, was to build trust. "If the teacher doesn't trust you, they just won't hear what you're telling them. They have to know you're trying to help them improve." And one of the easiest ways to build trust, he noted, in addition to meeting regularly and frequently, was to point out when a teacher has done something well.

"For example," Short told the department chairs, "I was in Jennifer Travers's music class earlier this week, and there was this wonderful moment when she was trying to teach two boys to read music and follow it with their voices. Normally, I'd expect the kids to be extremely self-conscious, but Jennifer made a game out of it and played it along with them. They were all laughing and having a wonderful time and learning to read music. I made a point of coming back as soon as the period ended to tell her what a great job she'd done.

"It's a little trickier if you see something that doesn't work and need to give adjusting feedback that could be interpreted negatively," Short continued. "In those cases, I make very sure the conversation is private, and I always start by saying something like, 'I'm impressed by your teaching, but I noticed something on which I think you could work.' And after I've explained what I observed, I usually end with a line like, 'Does that seem right to you? Can you work on that?'

"I've discovered," Short concluded, "that you have to give this feedback quickly. If more than a day passes, it threatens the trust factor, and the good feedback and the adjusting feedback lose their impact."

RESOURCES

Horstman, Mark. *The Effective Manager*. Hoboken, NJ: Wiley, 2016.

Scott, Kim. *Radical Candor*. New York, NY: St. Martin's Press, 2017.

24 Inclusivity and Diversity

Supporting intellectual growth through exposure to differing and challenging ideas

The role of education is to prepare students for a diverse and complex world. One of the school leader's responsibilities is to create a culture that encourages faculty and students to explore challenging concepts, experiment with new ideas, and collaborate with people of diverse backgrounds and viewpoints. A school leader should employ three strategies to create an open, tolerant culture:

1. Communicate diversity and inclusivity as a priority and create standards of conduct that prioritize this commitment
2. Provide training for faculty and staff to navigate difficult conversations
3. Develop a process for a curriculum review to determine whether there is diverse representation in instructional resources

Creating standards of conduct around how faculty and students should interact can help prioritize diversity and inclusivity as one of the school's strategic goals. These standards should articulate the ethical responsibilities of all to generate classrooms free of overt or inadvertent discrimination. Explicit standards will protect the most vulnerable students from undue harm. The school must also reinforce its commitment to diversity and inclusion through its enrollment and hiring practices.

Leaders should not assume that teachers have a deep understanding of how to enact inclusive practices and should provide them with professional-development opportunities that encourage inclusive strategies for their classrooms. While faculty and students may be uneasy with discussions of race, gender, or other differences, leaders should not shy away from their responsibility to ensure these conversations take place. A critical teaching skill is learning how to implement equitable and accountable discussion practices that provide students a structure for productive discourse.

One of the defining aspects of education is to challenge beliefs and ideas. In providing a diverse school curriculum, the leader accepts that being exposed to new and difficult concepts may cause students to feel upset and uncomfortable. The challenge brought by discussing diverse and challenging ideas, however, creates an extraordinary opportunity for students to learn and grow.

Research confirms that instructional content and practices that explicitly connect to a student's background can significantly accelerate many students' learning. A curriculum review can ensure students have an opportunity to engage with a variety of resources from a diverse range of perspectives. However, having diverse representation does not mean there needs to be an equal representation of every group. The goal should be to create a curriculum that is challenging, engaging, and diverse. With globalization has come a wealth of high quality resources from other cultures. The school's curriculum should utilize both classic works and excellent noncanonical resources that can support students' deeper understanding of the diverse world.

See also   Co-Teaching, Curriculum Leadership, Professional Development

DOI: 10.4324/9780429321641-24

CASE STUDY

Jim Short had hired Gloria Eastman as North High's first director of diversity, equity, and inclusion (DEI) after his first year at the school. While the student body seemed appropriately diverse for the demographics of the neighborhoods surrounding the school, the faculty was much less diverse. Short worried that despite general goodwill toward the families of color who sent their kids to the school, the overwhelming whiteness of the faculty was a systemic problem.

Jim and Gloria met weekly. Since she had arrived, she had organized several affinity groups for students of different ethnicities. She had done the same with members of the faculty and also organized two faculty workshops on DEI issues. When the hiring season began in the spring, Jim planned to have her represent the school at several regional hiring fairs. Today, however, she had a different topic for discussion at her weekly one-on-one.

"Jim, I was meeting with one of my student affinity groups, and they were talking about a book they were assigned in English class. It was a novel about kids in a small town, and they felt it was pretty unfair in its portrayal of families who had recently immigrated to the U.S."

"Did you talk to the teacher about it, Gloria?"

"I did. She said the book had been on the reading list for quite some time, and nobody had raised any concern. At the same time, she said she could see what the kids were talking about, and she wondered why she hadn't seen it herself. She actually became quite upset. I had to calm her down and assure her this kind of thing happened regularly. The world is changing, and materials that once worked well are now problematic."

"So, Jim," Gloria went on, "I think we need to do an audit of our curriculum and reading lists. It's unlikely this is the only problem we have."

"I agree, Gloria. It's important we organize this in a balanced way and make sure the whole community knows exactly what's going to happen. This is an election year, and we don't want to get caught up in the culture wars."

"Well, I'm happy to be a resource to whatever group you charge with doing the audit, Jim. But don't put me on the committee. People will be sure there's an agenda behind it."

"We need your expertise, Gloria."

"I'm happy to help you design the process and meet with the group when they need me. But believe me, Jim. If I'm on that group, people will be suspicious of the impartiality of the outcome."

RESOURCES

Forscher, Patrick S., Calvin K. Lai, Jordan R. Axt, Charles R. Ebersole, Michelle Herman, Patricia G. Devine, and Brian A. Nosek. "A Meta-Analysis of Procedures to Change Implicit Measures." *Journal of Personality and Social Psychology* 117, no. 3 (September 2019): 522–59. http://doi:10.1037/pspa0000160. (2019).

Ladson-Billings, Gloria. "Toward a Theory of Culturally Relevant Pedagogy." *American Educational Research Journal* 32, no. 3 (Autumn 1995): 465–91. Accessed January 2020. http://lmcreadinglist.pbworks.com/f/Ladson-Billings%20%281995%29.pdf.

25 Innovation Leadership

Creating the conditions for continuous improvement and transformational breakthroughs

Strong school leaders create efficient systems that bring consistency and stability to their schools, but they must also embrace change as they deal with a constant influx of new students and faculty and as instructional methodologies are regularly improved. Creating a culture of innovation requires a balance between stability and change in order to improve. The more standardized the systems created in a school, the harder it is to foster transformational shifts in thinking. To cultivate a culture of innovation, school leaders should:

1. Flatten hierarchies
2. Promote creativity
3. Increase diversity

Hierarchical organizations inhibit innovation. Schools that prioritize an innovative culture are nimbler because decision-making is decentralized and given to the people most familiar with an issue. Eliminating silos and encouraging cross-collaboration among individuals allows for synergies to flourish. However, this does not mean leaders should eliminate all managing hierarchies within the organization. Reporting structures are necessary for operational efficiency, but they should not inhibit communication. Empowering teams to define their own school-aligned goals allows innovative ideas, rather than hierarchical structures, to dictate how the school works. Teams that can devise, test, and assess innovative ways to meet their goals feel a sense of ownership of both the creation of ideas and their implementation.

Leaders cannot mandate a creative culture, but they can optimize the conditions that foster it. If faculty are encouraged to collaborate and share ideas and provided time to work together, creativity can flourish. However, creativity cannot be efficiently managed. Leaders should be cautious of the nirvana fallacy, which assumes an idea should be rejected if it doesn't provide a "perfect" solution to a problem. In their early stages, new ideas need time to mature and thus may work less well than more established ones. The creative process requires "play" and an open-mindedness to ideas that may seem flawed at the outset.

Diverse perspectives vastly increase the likelihood of innovation. If the same people are always asked to express their proposed solutions to challenges, they tend to create the same results. "Groupthink" is a notorious innovation killer. Bringing a diversity of perspectives allows a problem to be viewed from a multidimensional lens that may spark fresh new ideas.

See also Change Management, Piloting Crazy Ideas

RESOURCES

Christensen, Clayton M. *Disrupting Class: How Disruptive Innovation Will Change the Way the World Learns.* New York, NY: McGraw-Hill, 2008.

Pisano, Gary P. "The Hard Truth About Innovative Cultures." *Harvard Business Review* 97, no. 1 (January–February 2019): 62–71.

DOI: 10.4324/9780429321641-25

CASE STUDY

It always amazed Jim Short how a minor bureaucratic annoyance, gradually embedded in the hierarchy of a school, could become a major problem. Such was the case at North High with what was known as "the increment system." AP teachers argued their courses were more demanding than the standard curriculum and that the students who took them should receive an increment to their academic average simply for entering the more demanding AP track. Over time, the increments had expanded beyond just AP and were now a complex system, controlled by a powerful assistant principal; worse, the process encouraged every student to try to "game" the system.

Short wanted the increment system revised, if not eliminated. But given its tradition and importance to students and their parents, he wanted substantial faculty support before he moved. He met with the assistant principal who oversaw the system and explained what he planned to do. He was going to create a tiger team to revise the increment system over the course of the school year. That team had to look at increment systems in other schools, as well as in schools that had given up increments. He wanted students included in the process in addition to at least a couple of parents. He was asking the assistant principal to organize the tiger team and support it but not to lead it or be a part of the team's discussions.

Initially, the assistant principal did not take this news well; but as he thought about it, he realized there was some wisdom in Short's suggestion, and he agreed to the role of hands-off organizer. He and Short immediately began to suggest potential individuals for the team. "We need team members who can play well together and not try to turn the team's work into an effort to gain advantage for their department or discipline," Short said, and with those criteria, they began to select the tiger team.

Short never missed a chance to inform the faculty, parents, and students of what was underway. He said he wanted the new system to be simple, fair, and educationally significant. To make sure that happened, he reserved the decision to implement the new system for himself.

After a couple of months of meetings, Short began to get reports that the tiger team was making progress. Tiger team members were advocating in their departments for change and starting to convince the colleagues who clung to the old system. The lack of hierarchy in the tiger team contributed to a positive spirit, and by the end of the year, Short had a recommendation to eliminate the increment system that he could enthusiastically support.

26 Instructional Coaching
Improving faculty pedagogical practices

The main goal of instructional coaching is to improve pedagogical practice in teachers and thus student learning, growth, and achievement. Like all school-improvement strategies, instructional coaching should be aligned to the organization's goals.

All instructional coaches should be master classroom teachers and have the skills, such as collaboration, communication, and creativity, necessary for teacher leadership. Some instructional coaches are teacher leaders who work alongside the classroom teacher, while others may be outside consultants. Increasingly, however, school leaders have taken on the dual role of manager and instructional coach. There are myriad upsides to this arrangement. Administrators with an understanding of classroom culture and teacher quality are better equipped to align teacher practice to school goals. Also, using school administrators as instructional coaches allows for a more efficient allocation of budgetary resources.

Jim Knight describes three distinct approaches to instructional coaching: facilitative, directive, and dialogical. "Facilitative" is the most hands-off approach; the coach listens and follows a line of inquiry so the teacher can solve their own problems. "Directive" is a prescriptive method of coaching that requires the coach to have expert instructional knowledge. "Dialogical" coaching is a blend of both types. While all three approaches have their purpose and proponents, dialogical coaching is the preferred method in most situations.

Dialogical coaching requires the coach to act as a thought partner for the teacher. In this modality, the coach has two main jobs. The first is to use inquiry to engage the teacher in conversations about their practice and to draw out the knowledge and expertise the teacher already possesses. The second is to use advocacy to provide strategies, content knowledge, and constructive feedback to the teacher. In dialogical coaching, the coach can share their opinions about what might work best in the classroom, but decision-making ultimately resides with the teacher. The coach's main goal is to support the teacher's thinking so they can make informed instructional decisions.

Instructional coaches employ many different tools when they are coaching teachers. These include classroom observation, lesson modeling, videotaping of instruction, goal setting, data collection and analysis, and one-on-one conversations. The types of tools a coach chooses to use depend greatly on the approach being employed and the assessment of the teacher's understanding of the pedagogy in question. While an instructional coach's main role is to support individual teachers in the classroom, they also can provide broader coaching and professional-development opportunities across schools and school districts.

See also   Developmental Coaching, Instructional Rounds, Mentorship

RESOURCES

Aguilar, Elena. *The Art of Coaching*. Hoboken, NJ: Jossey-Bass, 2013.
Knight, Jim. *The Impact Cycle*. Thousand Oaks, CA: Corwin, 2018.

DOI: 10.4324/9780429321641-26

Jim Short found, when he became the principal of North High, that he missed being a classroom teacher. However, he also found that coaching teachers to become better teachers and helping new teachers to enter the profession successfully was immensely satisfying. Coaching his faculty gave him insights into how the school was working and added to his credibility with both faculty and students.

Right now, Short was focusing on Ms. Hynes, a history teacher new to North High but with several years of previous teaching experience. Earlier in the week, Short had visited two ninth-grade history classes Ms. Hynes had taught, and today, they were having their first one-on-one coaching session.

"Let me start by putting you at ease," Short began. "I thought you did well in both classes. The second class has a couple of kids who appear to have some focus issues, but you didn't let that distract you, and you brought them along in the discussion. I liked that you didn't just lecture. You got a real discussion going."

Short could see Ms. Hynes relaxing as he spoke. "What did you feel worked best?" he asked.

"I thought they really enjoyed the 15 minutes we spent playing Jeopardy with facts about the Constitution. That seemed to perk up the whole class."

"I agree, that did work well for most of the students. Did you see any problems with it?"

Ms. Hynes thought for a minute. "I didn't notice this at the time, but I realize now none of the ESL students took part."

"I noticed that too, "Short said. "Maybe they weren't familiar with the format of the TV show?"

"Or maybe they didn't understand the significance of the Constitution," Ms. Hynes said. "I need to look into that. Maybe that game has drawbacks."

"Well, it was a clever idea," Short replied. "And you had obviously done a lot of preparation to make it happen. Sometimes, however, good ideas have unintended consequences. When you hit one of those spots, you need to think about whether the original idea needs modification or if maybe it can't be made to work. That's your decision, but you should know that if I spot something I think needs more work, I'll bring it to your attention. I have a lot of confidence in your ability to take a good idea and make it better."

27 Instructional Rounds

A process of observation, analysis, and discussion used to improve student learning at scale

The practice of instructional rounds derives from medical rounds used in teaching hospitals. In medical rounds, physicians visit patients, analyze their charts, and discuss possible treatment options. This process creates a strong foundational knowledge base among colleagues and builds professional norms around the expected quality of practice. In schools, instructional rounds similarly require that educators observe classrooms and use data about teaching practice to deepen their understanding of classroom instruction. However, the purpose of instructional rounds in schools is not only to build expertise and understanding but to move an entire school or district toward a shared coherent strategy of school improvement.

Instructional rounds are different in scope from classroom walkthroughs and peer observations. Walkthroughs and observations are meant to diagnose individual classroom issues and provide feedback to individual teachers. By contrast, instructional rounds are designed to improve instruction schoolwide and are rarely conducted with the frequency of walkthroughs. They are meant to support pedagogical improvement *at scale*. Action steps after instructional rounds might be the launch of a whole-school professional-development initiative or a reallocation of resources to support a particular instructional strategy throughout a school district.

Instructional rounds require a significant time commitment. In a typical rounds process, a group of educators is chosen to participate in a full- or half-day exercise. The size of the group is important; usually a group of no fewer than five and no more than twenty is appropriate. The number of classrooms observed by the participants depends greatly on the question being asked but should be sufficient for participants to get a sense of the instructional practice happening across the entire school. On average, there should not be more than three to five observers in any one classroom at a given time.

After a problem of practice is identified, the group should collect classroom observations and follow with time for group analysis. At the end of the instructional rounds process, the group should make recommendations about potential next steps. Next steps should be viewed in the context of the school or school district as a whole and should be directed to best leverage resources to support instruction at scale.

Instructional rounds are a cyclical process that is tied to a school's goals and improvement plan. They are meant to be inquiry based rather than evaluative, so the frequency of rounds depends greatly on the group's line of inquiry and diagnosis of the issue. Some school groups do rounds biweekly. Others do rounds monthly or once a semester. Alignment to school goals, participant engagement, and the complexity and urgency of the problem of practice will all determine the frequency of the rounds.

See also   Change Management, Curriculum Leadership

RESOURCES

City, Elizabeth A., Richard F. Elmore, Sarah E. Fiarman, and Lee Teitel. *Instructional Rounds in Education: A Network Approach to Improving Teaching and Learning*, 6th ed. Cambridge, MA: Harvard Education Press, 2009.

DOI: 10.4324/9780429321641-27

CASE STUDY

North High had gone through an unusual number of leadership changes in the six years before Jim Short had been named principal. Talking to faculty and his new administrative team, it seemed to him that while the staff could identify many issues that needed attention, there was no strategy for setting priorities and identifying the big tasks they needed to tackle.

Short decided to try implementing the process of instructional rounds as a way to sort out what mattered and establish both some immediate changes and simultaneously a process to establish priorities for the future.

He began by recruiting his team. He settled on sixteen people, including several senior faculty and members of his administrative team, as well as two other principals and faculty and administrators from the other high schools. The superintendent's office sent a representative. Before they began, Short reviewed the goal of instructional rounds with the whole team and asked their commitment to the principle that the goal was pedagogical improvement at scale, not individual evaluation of teachers.

Short decided to focus the first instructional round on the new mathematics curriculum North High had introduced a year before. This was a problem-based curriculum with a significant discovery component. Short had heard lots of complaints from parents and faculty that the students were "confused" by the new curriculum. He divided his team into four groups of four and published a detailed schedule for the teams to visit all of North's math classes.

On the scheduled day, Short convened his sixteen volunteers and reviewed the goals of the instructional round. After the classroom visits were completed, the entire group reconvened and shared their observations. Short asked them first to just report what they observed, not to suggest change. It soon became clear that all the math classes were very teacher centered. Only one team reported they had observed the students doing any independent group work. The group concluded that the lack of independent work might hamper the students from feeling personal ownership of the concepts they were learning. After more discussion, the group agreed to recommend that the math teachers incorporate more independent group work into their instruction.

Short thanked the team and scheduled the next instructional round in two months' time.

28   Leadership Team

The team ultimately accountable for student learning and well-being

Organizations need a highly functional leadership team to succeed. But merely having a group of leaders call themselves a "team" does not ensure they will work well together. The first step to creating an effective leadership team is to hire the best people for the job. By "best," the team leader must consider:

1. The leadership mindset of each team member
2. The context and school environment the team will need to navigate

Leadership mindset is hugely important to finding the best candidate for the team. Each new leadership team member will need to possess two essential traits: mission alignment and the ability to accept feedback. Without mission alignment, the leadership team will be challenged to agree upon a vision and strategic plan for the school. For the team to continuously improve and make progress toward a shared vision, each team member will need to be open to receiving constructive feedback. A leadership team that does not possess these necessary traits will be unable to lead successfully.

If the team possesses the right leadership mindset, the school environment will be the other factor to consider. The team leader needs to understand what the team must do for the school to be successful. If the school is a start-up, the best leadership team may be great at creating and operationalizing new systems. If the school is well established, the ideal team may be of leaders who can ensure school traditions are upheld and families and faculty feel well supported. Conversely, if the school is in a turnaround situation, the best team may be crisis managers who can get quick results in a highly stressful environment. Too often, if the right candidate has not emerged at the beginning of a school year, school leaders will feel pressure to hire team members who don't possess the right mindset or skill set. It is better to leave a vacancy than to hire a leader who is a bad fit for a particular context.

Once the right team is on board, leaders must invest in a team culture focused on mission, goals, strategies, and measurement. A great leadership team works hard to create a high level of trust and invests in the school's overall mission through strategic planning and communication to faculty and families. Being explicit about yearly school goals and cascading these goals into smaller team objectives are important ways the leadership team can communicate a "one team" culture. They should continually revisit these shared goals and hold each other, as well as the broader faculty, accountable to making progress on their commitments.

See also   School Climate, Prioritization

RESOURCES

Katzenbach, Jon R., and Douglas K. Smith. *The Wisdom of Teams: Creating the High-Performance Organization*, repr. Cambridge, MA: Harvard Business Review Press, 2015.

Lencioni, Patrick. *The Five Dysfunctions of a Team*. San Francisco, CA: Jossey-Bass, 2002.

Senge, Peter M. *The Fifth Discipline: The Art and Practice of the Learning Organization*, rev. ed. 1990; repr. New York, NY: Doubleday, 2006.

DOI: 10.4324/9780429321641-28

CASE STUDY

Jim Short sometimes fantasized about starting a new school so he could hire his leadership team from scratch. But like most school principals, Short had to both educate and encourage the team he inherited to internalize a common sense of mission and to develop trust and communication skills so every team member added to the overall performance of the whole team.

A good team started, Short believed, with good communication and a strong routine. He had a team meeting once a week, which generally lasted 90 minutes. Part of the agenda dealt with the crises that had arisen during the week; part focused on long-term problems and goals and their short-term implications; and part, the most important part from Short's point of view, focused on concerns raised by team members. Every four to six weeks, Short devoted a meeting to professional development, sometimes with a shared reading, sometimes with an expert presenter. Instructional rounds, a new experience for some team members, helped to focus the team on the real mission of North High—the educational success of its students.

Short took seriously his responsibility to be a role model. He took very seriously the regular one-on-ones he had with each of his direct reports and listened carefully to their concerns. The team wouldn't be truthful with him if he weren't truthful with them. If he met failure or disappointment with anger, no one would risk admitting when things went badly. Over time, Short trusted—and his experience confirmed this instinct—that his behavior could inspire trust among his leadership colleagues. Sometimes a leader Short "inherited" didn't work out, but more often than not, the old team grew into a new team under his leadership.

29 Meeting Facilitation
Running productive meetings

Skillful meeting facilitation ensures a school team works cohesively, increases productivity, encourages new and innovative ideas, and makes progress on intended goals. By contrast, poorly facilitated meetings waste valuable time, frustrate those involved, and are a detriment to positive school culture.

It is important to understand that preparation is essential to an effective meeting. Four important components need to be included when planning for every meeting:

1. Purpose and outcomes
2. Agenda
3. Action items
4. Process

The meeting leader should clearly articulate the purpose of the team meeting, ideally before the meeting convenes. Plan a meeting with an outcome aligned to its purpose and that answers the question, What will be different at the end of the meeting? For example, if the purpose of the meeting is to design a summer professional-development experience for teachers, some potential outcomes might be to generate ideas for courses and activities, designate a subteam to handle the logistics, develop an agenda for the week, or all of the above.

A well-thought-out agenda is the cornerstone of a great meeting. It serves as a road map for the participants. Agendas can be designed by the facilitator or can be co-constructed by the facilitator and the participants but should be shared ahead of time if possible. In an agenda, the purpose, outcomes, roles, and action items should be clearly listed. It is also useful to designate a time frame for each agenda item.

Most meetings should end with action items for the group. Even if the purpose of the meeting is to generate ideas or gain understanding about a topic, it is still important to clearly articulate next steps. Action items are tasks, assigned to one or more of the meeting participants, that have a deadline for completion so the group is aware of who is doing what next. Meeting notes need to capture these assignments for follow-up.

The last crucial element to facilitate a great meeting is to attend to its process as much as its content. Beginning the meeting with an exercise to help the participants get to know one another can help break the ice. Likewise, starting the meeting with a few process agreements can help create boundaries and establish rules to ensure productivity. Agreement statements like "assume positive intent" or "use technology to enhance, not distract from, the meeting goals" can be useful. Finally, clear roles for some members of the meeting—notetaker, timekeeper, and person designated to email members about follow-up action items—will facilitate the orderly process of the meeting.

See also Communication Excellence

RESOURCES

Miranda, Shalla M., and Robert P. Bostrom. "Meeting Facilitation: Process Versus Content Interventions." *The Journal of Management Information Systems* 15, no. 4 (1999): 89–114. https://doi.org/10.1080/07421222.1999.11518223.

DOI: 10.4324/9780429321641-29

CASE STUDY

When Jim Short arrived at North High, he learned his senior staff had a weekly meeting. As he was getting to know his new colleagues, he asked them about the meeting and if it was helpful. "Oh, it's great to get together," one colleague told him. "The principal usually starts the meeting by asking us what's going on, and people bring up issues if they have them. But really, not much happens; it's mostly hang-out time."

Short resolved to tighten up the meeting process. Two days before his first senior staff meeting, he sent out a memo with an agenda. In addition, he told his staff that if they had any points they wanted to add to the agenda, they should email those topics to him at least twenty-four hours before the meeting. Two of the agenda items involved financial decisions, and he emailed his business manager to alert him to be ready for that discussion.

Short prepared a brief statement of purpose as the first item on his agenda: "The senior staff will meet weekly for the purpose of making decisions that require broad administrative input and for sharing critical information that all senior staff need to know." He knew hang-out time was important for morale, but he resolved to meet that need when the school itself wasn't in session.

As the first meeting began, Short proposed a brief warm-up exercise: "Let's go around the table and everyone do thirty seconds on what gave you the most fun on summer break." He handed a bell to the person next to him. "Bill, you be the timekeeper; ring it when people have hit thirty seconds!" The staff was caught off guard, but Short went first, and the bell rang before he had barely started. By the end, everyone was laughing and shouting single words: "Golf! Swimming! Hot dogs!"

Short had invited his assistant to come to the meeting and take notes. He promised to share a copy of these notes with the entire senior staff and said the notes would highlight the individual staff responsibilities assigned in the meeting. "As a matter of course," he said, "be prepared to update us on your outstanding projects when we meet."

30 Mentorship
Assigning experienced educators to guide novice teachers

The first year of teaching can be the hardest for new teachers, as they are asked to plan, prepare, and show skill proficiency with students on the first day of school. This challenge is evidenced by the rate that new teachers leave the profession—a staggering 10% after their first year and nearly 50% within five years. To address this attrition dilemma, school leaders should create a mentorship program to support all new teachers in their school. Leaders should consider three important factors when establishing a mentorship program for new teachers:

1. Mentorship expectations
2. Mentor quality
3. Mentor support

Mentorship is a program that guides new teachers through their entire first year. School leaders should clearly articulate that a mentor's chief purpose is to support the new teacher, not to manage or direct them. Without clear guidance, a mentor and mentee may have different expectations for the mentoring relationship, and the quality of the mentoring may be diminished. There are other skills a mentor can bring to the mentorship role—developmental and instructional coaching. However, if a school leader wishes a mentor to take on additional coaching responsibilities, these modifications can be included but should not conflict with their principal responsibilities. Mentorship should always be chiefly about mentees' growth and never an evaluative nor supervisory role.

Leaders need to choose their mentors carefully to ensure they have the proper disposition. Because a mentor's chief purpose is to guide novice teachers through the challenges of their first year of teaching, these experienced faculty need to be committed and trusting advisors who can understand and prioritize the unique development of beginning teachers. Some mentees may be open to bringing up issues and asking for help, while others may be defensive and reluctant to share their problems and challenges. Trust building requires the mentor to have regularly scheduled one-on-one conversations with their mentees in which the mentee can freely raise issues they would like to discuss. This time should be an open forum for the mentee and not a space where the mentor sets the agenda and drives the conversation.

To make a strong statement about the importance of the work of mentorship, mentors should be given release time from extra duties. School leaders need to communicate frequently with their mentors to ensure they know how the novice teachers are progressing and if they require extra support or resources.

Mentorship is one component of a comprehensive induction program and should be combined with an onboarding process, instructional coaching, and an induction support group for new teachers.

See also   Developmental Coaching, Instructional Coaching, New Teacher Induction

RESOURCES

Ingersoll, Richard, and Michael Strong. "The Impact of Induction and Mentoring Programs for Beginning Teachers: A Critical Review of the Research." *Review of Educational Research* 81, no. 2 (2011): 201–33. https://doi.org/10.3102/0034654311403323.

DOI: 10.4324/9780429321641-30

CASE STUDY

Jim Short assigned each of his new teachers a mentor. Research and personal experience showed that having a mentor reduced new teacher attrition significantly. Many of his senior faculty enjoyed being mentors, and Short had found that if there were a lot of new faculty, experienced mentors could take on two or even three mentees. Short liked to stay in touch with the mentors, especially in the first few months of school, and scheduled short chats with them once every two weeks during the fall term.

Sam Delgado, an English teacher, was mentoring Curt Smart, a new foreign languages instructor. Although he was an experienced teacher, this was the first time Delgado had been a mentor. He leapt at the chance to have his study hall assignment cut in return for mentoring. But Delgado was having trouble mentoring Smart. He felt Smart was ignoring his advice and asking questions that made Delgado uncomfortable.

"I gave Curt a syllabus of all the things we were going to talk about this fall," Delgado said. "I started with academic records and grading, and I asked him to look up the records of a couple of his kids, and we'd go through them. Standard stuff. But he wants to talk about Evelyn Landis, his department chair. He's having some kind of problem with her, but I'm not going there."

"Any idea what sort of problem?" Short asked.

"He's teaching mostly ninth grade, and he doesn't think Evelyn is giving him credit for all his graduate work. He'd like an advanced class."

"Do you think he's up to that?" Short asked.

"I really don't know; it's not my field."

"Have you talked to Evelyn to find out how Curt is doing?" Short asked.

"No, I haven't. Is that part of what I'm supposed to do?"

"Sam," Short replied, "I want you to do a couple of things as a mentor. I want you to be a good friend to Curt and build trust with him. I want him to be able to tell you what's bothering him, even if it delays discussing the items on your syllabus. And I want you to help him be a great teacher. Maybe he's right. Maybe he could do more advanced classes, but the first thing you need to know before you advise him is whether he's doing well with the ninth-graders Evelyn assigned him."

Koki, Stan. "The Role of Teacher Mentoring in Educational Reform." PREL Briefing Paper. Honolulu, HI: Pacific Resources for Education and Learning, 1997. www.nmu.edu/Webb/ArchivedHTML/UPCED/mentoring/docs/Role-mentor.pdf.

West, Andrew. "A Framework for Conceptualizing Models of Mentoring in Educational Settings." *International Journal of Leadership and Change* 4 no. 1 (2016): Article 11. https://digitalcommons.wku.edu/ijlc/vol4/iss1/11.

31 Mission and Vision

Articulations of an organization's purpose, values, and goals

To successfully attract students and educators, it is important for a school to communicate what it wants to achieve and who it needs to serve. If it does so, students, faculty, and families can better understand the school's values and whether those values align with their beliefs about learning. Mission and vision statements articulate a school's purpose to the school community as well as inspire the community's members.

In articulating the school's purpose, a mission statement defines why the organization exists and the impact it wants to make. A key component of a good mission statement is that it operationalizes the organization's goals. It should never indulge in superfluous self-congratulation. Mission statements should be succinct and to the point. As a general rule, a mission statement should not exceed two to three sentences in length.

A vision statement answers the question, "What does success look like?" It projects the organization's hopes into the future. Its purpose is to uplift and inspire. Vision statements should emphasize the unique characteristics of the school that set it apart from schools that others may view as similar. It is less important for vision statements to be concise, since crafting a vision that resonates with the reader is key. For school faculty, a strong vision statement can shape their understanding of why they chose to work at this particular school.

School mission and vision statements are often created by the founding faculty and administration. To create a founding mission or vision statement, key leaders and stakeholders may meet to brainstorm, ideate, and identify many possible values in resonant words and phrases. This initial "whiteboard" exercise is immediately followed by repeatedly editing and distilling the statement into draft language for broader community review and finalization. Once established, these statements should be communicated to the school community. By doing so, the founding leadership of the school can shape the school culture and create a set of core values to guide all members of the school community.

There are many ways a school leader can utilize mission and vision statements. Within a school, they can be used to guide the leadership team's strategy in moments of change within the organization. As a form of professional development for faculty, school leaders can work with educator teams to unpack the mission statement, analyzing its terms to bring to life what they mean to the contemporary school. They can also be critically helpful when soliciting outside support, resources, or partnerships, as they can clearly communicate to outsiders the school's purpose, beliefs, and values.

See also   Goal Setting, Leadership Team, School Climate

RESOURCES

Owens, Ben. "Do You Know Your School's Vision? Tips on Making a Meaningful Mission Statement." *Education Week*, November 21, 2017.

DOI: 10.4324/9780429321641-31

CASE STUDY

Jim Short pondered the mission of his school district: "Our curriculum is designed to help students develop intellectually, physically, emotionally, ethically, aesthetically, and socially. We encourage students to become active, engaged learners and responsible citizens." In general, he thought it was a good mission statement, although it had been drafted when the city was considerably less diverse than it was today. Short wished the mission statement made an explicit goal of celebrating what a diverse community North High had become.

Practically, the school district really only focused on the first part of the mission. Intellectual development, as measured in performance on standardized exams and in college placement, was a big topic at the school board and in the community. And while other aspects of student development—"physically, emotionally, ethically, aesthetically, and socially"—all figured into intellectual development, they were unique developmental properties as well.

Short wished the district were doing some measurement of how well the North High students were doing in the realms beyond intellectual development.

Short talked it over with his senior staff. "I think we're underleveraging our mission statement by just looking at what the district feels is the most important," he said. "We can't change that mission statement; the district owns it. But even if they choose to focus on just one part of the mission, we can pay some attention to its other parts. Let's figure out how to do that."

With the approval of the superintendent, Short put together faculty-led teams to brainstorm some growth indicators for the five areas the district's mission failed to assess. To gain broad support, he added a few parents to each of the teams. "We can't ignore the parents' vision of what they want their kids to become," Short said. Two students were also added to each team. Each team was asked to develop three to five well-defined, highly measurable characteristics that could be used to define progress in each of the other five parts of the mission.

After months of discussion, Short and the faculty reached consensus on the variables they would add to their annual tracking of intellectual development. Short publicized their work in a presentation called "Measures of Excellence," which he gave to students, parents, and other schools in the district. Slowly, the conversation about mission began to expand as other principals saw the success Short was having with his new measures.

32 Networking
Cultivating essential relationships for strategic success

Most school leaders are selected for leadership because they are outgoing and good at building relationships. In the early days of a leader's tenure, this skill becomes critical, since much of the inner workings of schools and school systems is not written down but passed along through conversation. Thus, having networks in which a school leader can get reliable information and develop alliances is critical to survival. School leaders access three common types of networks:

1. Community networks
2. Professional networks
3. Supportive or developmental networks

Community networks are often the most overlooked and simultaneously the most important. Usually, they are assembled by the school leader as they become acquainted with the town that supports their school. It is a wise allocation of a new school leader's time to visit key community leaders: mayor, police chief, fire chief, religious leaders, and newspaper editors. Having access to these individuals can be of tremendous help to a school leader. To have reliable access, the leader must cultivate personal relationships. Inviting the police chief to a school event, for example, can move a relationship beyond the simply transactional.

Professional networks are important sources of regional and national information, techniques, and new developments that can enhance a leader's performance. Many regional school organizations invite the membership of principals and superintendents and provide professional support as well as workshops on new developments that school leaders can bring back to their home communities.

In the last several decades, there has been great growth in professional organizations that provide developmental networks for cohorts who may face special challenges in entering long-established school leadership groups—women and people of color. These organizations provide training, support, and introduction to senior professionals who can mentor developing leaders.

In today's world, email and videoconferencing offer efficient and low-cost means of exchanging information and having meetings that simulate face-to-face discussion. Both individuals and organizations can also use social networks to provide efficient connections. These technologies have all expanded the power of professional and developmental networks to connect their membership with each other.

Times of crisis often demonstrate the importance of having networks that support the leader and their organization. When a school is vandalized, a teacher is hurt in a car accident, or a student's family suffers a tragedy, accessing the community network can have enormous impact. Likewise, when parents complain to the school board about a curricular change, the support of a professional or developmental network can provide information and a national perspective on the appropriateness of the change. Wise school leaders develop their networks carefully and participate in them actively for their personal benefit and for the benefit of their organization.

See also Principal Practices

DOI: 10.4324/9780429321641-32

CASE STUDY

Jim Short had been friends with Tim Watts for some years before Watts took the job of trying to turn around a troubled school. After Watts's first two years as principal, the turnaround was going amazingly well, and Short was impressed. What surprised him was that he never saw Watts at any meetings of the state principals' association.

When they next got together for lunch, he asked Watts about it.

"I know I should go," said Watts, "but I never feel like I have the time. This project—starting a science-technology magnet program—has really taken time. And I'm not sure I really need to hang out with a bunch of overworked school principals."

"I can understand that, Tim. In fact, I assumed that would be your answer. But I think you ought to think about it a little more. Let me ask you another question. How well do you know the mayor, the fire chief, and the police chief?"

"I've met them all. I guess that's it."

"Call 'em by their first names?"

"Can't say that I do."

"Will they take a call from you?"

"Maybe . . . maybe not."

"You need to work on your network, Tim. I visit the police chief every couple of months. Same with the fire chief. I know the mayor, although I don't visit him that often. These relationships really help when you have a crisis!

"Let's go back to the principals' organization, Tim. I go to those luncheons regularly. I never come home without having picked up a good idea from somebody. And when I run into a problem, there's always someone who has gone through it before whom I can call to get some advice."

"Ah, you're making me feel guilty, Jim. I know there are a lot of good people who go to those meetings, and I would learn a lot. But I just haven't found the motivation yet to go."

"And I know you're a bit of a loner, Tim. That's probably why you're good at taking on troubled schools. But the value of these organizations isn't just a social one, although I have made some good friends in them. Take your rebooting of your school as a sci-tech magnet. You know there's a national organization of magnet schools. Are you in that network?"

"Bet you can guess the answer to that, Jim."

"Well, I think you ought to get into that network. There are a lot of magnet schools around the country, and I'm sure the information you get and the contacts you make will be worth the price of admission."

"You've convinced me, Jim! Let me buy you lunch."

RESOURCES

Chapman, Christopher, and Mark Hadfield. "School-Based Networking for Educational Change." In *Second International Handbook of Educational Change* (*Springer International Handbooks of Education* 23, September 2010), 765–80. New York, NY: Springer Publishing. http://dx.doi.org/10.1007/978-90-481-2660-6_43.

Livingston, David. "Seven Questions of Networking." *School Administrator* 64, no. 4 (April 2007): 26–32.

33 New Teacher Induction

Supporting novice teachers with orientation, guidance, and mentoring

Approximately 44% of teachers leave within the first five years of teaching (with just under 10% leaving before the end of their first year). Given this sobering statistic, a well-executed induction plan can alleviate some of the initial stressors while novice teachers learn how to teach and hone their practice. Induction programs prioritize high-leverage instructional practices while acclimating the new teachers to the school culture. They should carefully organize how teachers will learn the necessary systems, pedagogy, curriculum planning, management, and assessment over the year. There are three major supports that new teachers require at the beginning of their careers that will set them up for success in teaching:

1. Onboarding
2. Mentorship
3. Induction group

Induction should begin with an onboarding period before the start of the school year. This usually happens in late summer and may occur with the entire returning staff or be reserved for only new hires. Onboarding is a good opportunity for new teachers to take a deep dive into the school's mission and vision and get oriented to the school building. It is also a time to introduce the school's curriculum and lesson- and unit-planning methodology, as well as other school systems.

The next phase of induction occurs a few days before the school year begins. This is the ideal time to assign new teachers a mentor to be their guide throughout the year. A new teacher mentor should be a person who has solid instructional experience, is well versed in the school culture, and is enthusiastic about sharing their expertise with a junior colleague. It is essential that every new teacher have a reliable person to whom they can turn when they have logistical questions or need instructional support. In the first few days before the start of the year, the mentor can assist their mentee by introducing them to returning staff members, helping them gather resources, and setting up their classrooms.

As soon as the year begins, it is important to schedule new faculty to participate in an induction support group that meets regularly. As they become more acclimated to teaching and have a basic understanding of the school culture, they will develop confidence in their new roles. An induction support group will allow them to explore their new teaching role; and as the year unfolds, they will have more mental space to discuss specific issues—both methodological and theoretical. Asking teachers what issues are important to them and planning sessions around those ideas will help teachers grow and develop into capable professionals.

See also   Developmental Coaching, Mentorship, School Climate

RESOURCES

Ingersoll, Richard M., Lisa Merrill, Daniel Stuckey, and Gregory Collins. "Seven Trends: The Transformation of the Teaching Force – Updated October 2018." *CPRE Research Reports* #RR 2018–2 (October 2018). Philadelphia, PA: Consortium for Policy Research in Education, University of Pennsylvania.

DOI: 10.4324/9780429321641-33

CASE STUDY

One of the aspects of North High School Jim Short knew he had to change as soon as he took over as principal was the minimal effort expended on preparing new teachers to understand the culture of the school and the many responsibilities teachers undertook. Short thought back somewhat bitterly to his own first teaching experience. That school had had a one-day orientation for new faculty on the day before school started. At the last minute, a near brush from a September hurricane forced the cancellation of orientation. Short began the school year never having seen his classroom. He remembered how embarrassed he felt when he had to ask students for directions to the cafeteria.

Short planned a comprehensive onboarding program and published his plan for the new *and* returning faculty. It began with a three-day program in late June with the new faculty and all department chairs and senior administrative staff. The goal of this program was to introduce the new faculty to philosophical issues, such as the school mission, as well as practical issues, such as grading policy. There was plenty of time in the schedule for the new faculty to meet their colleagues.

Short told the new faculty that when they returned to campus, three days before the students arrived, they would each be assigned a mentor. The role of the mentor would be to provide supportive, friendly advice but not to evaluate performance. The mentors would all be experienced faculty, teaching in a different department from their mentee. Mentors were expected to meet with their mentees at least once every two weeks during the mentee's first year.

When the new faculty arrived on campus before the start of school, their meeting agenda became practical: how to access the school's technology, detailed discussions of grade reporting and attendance, and how to handle discipline issues. Short hosted a welcome dinner for the new faculty and their mentors. He also announced he would meet the new faculty once a month to introduce timely issues and to hear their questions and concerns. As he walked the halls on the first day of school and saw the new faculty greeting their students, he thought about how different their first day of teaching was from his.

Villani, Susan. *Mentoring Programs for New Teachers: Models of Induction and Support*, 2nd ed. Thousand Oaks, CA: Corwin, 2019.

34   One-on-One (O3) Meeting
Regular communication with a direct report

A one-on-one (O3) is the meeting in which a supervisor and a direct report communicate on a regular basis. To assess the direct report's strengths and weaknesses, the supervisor must get them to openly speak about their understanding of organizational goals, engagement in their work, successes, and failures along the way. Open communication builds trust so direct reports feel comfortable sharing their work and can communicate where they need support.

During an O3, the direct report should ask questions, get feedback on how they are doing, and request the support they need to be successful. The supervisor's primary role in these meetings is to listen, ask clarifying questions, and provide guidance where necessary. They need to understand that the direct report's issues take precedence and allow the direct report to set the agenda. Many supervisors wrongly create agendas for their direct reports with the intention of modeling strong organizational skills. If the supervisor shares an agenda in advance of the O3 meeting, the direct report will always default to that agenda and will not prioritize their own. Ideally, a 30-minute O3 should be structured like this:

- The first 10 minutes should be about the direct report's work
- The next 10 minutes should be the response to and support of what the direct identifies as the area(s) of need
- The last 10 minutes should focus on the direct report's future and areas of professional growth

O3s should be regularly scheduled, either weekly or biweekly. In small schools, weekly is ideal, but biweekly may be necessary if a supervisor supports more than ten teachers. The reason to schedule the weekly is to allow for consistent, regular contact so the direct report can feel supported and a relationship can be built. Half an hour should be enough time for a consistent, weekly O3. However, if the O3 is scheduled biweekly, 45 minutes may be more appropriate. O3s should not go over 45 minutes, however, even if there are items on the agenda left to discuss; longer O3s can begin to feel like a performance review rather than a check-in.

Supervisors in larger schools may require their direct reports to schedule weekly or biweekly check-ins with other people (such as an instructional coach, department chair, or mentor). However, each direct report needs to have an opportunity for a regular, consistent touch point through which they can receive support and guidance.

See also   In-the-Moment Feedback, School Climate

RESOURCES

Boyatzis, Richard E., and Annie McKee. *Resonant Leadership: Renewing Yourself and Connecting with Others Through Mindfulness, Hope, and Compassion.* Boston, MA: Harvard Business School Press, 2005.

Horstman, Mark. *The Effective Manager.* Hoboken, NJ: Wiley, 2016.

DOI: 10.4324/9780429321641-34

CASE STUDY

Jim Short's predecessor at North High disliked meetings and believed most educators agreed with him. Short knew that unnecessary meetings or badly organized ones were a blight on any organization, but he believed leaders needed to meet regularly with their direct reports to build morale and improve the school's capacity to do its work.

Early in his tenure, he raised the topic at a senior staff meeting: "I'd like everybody to schedule weekly 30-minute one-on-one meetings with their direct reports," Short announced. "The purpose of these meetings is to hear from your reports what their concerns are. You need to remember these are meetings designed to support them. They aren't training sessions."

A month later, Short put the subject of the O3s on his weekly staff agenda. He said he wanted to hear from everyone how these meetings were going. When the group convened, Short called on Irene Stefanick, head of special education, to lead off the discussion.

"Well, "Stefanick said, "this has been a new experience for me and, I think, for the people who work for me as well. In general, I trust people to do a good job, and these meetings are making people feel as if I don't trust them."

"That's not supposed to happen," said Short. "Irene, tell us how the meeting goes. How do you start it off?"

"I have an agenda," Stefanick replied. "I ask them to review their goals for the week and then summarize how they are doing in meeting those goals. When there's a shortfall, and nobody's perfect, we talk about what needs to be done to strengthen that area. And like I said, it really feels as though it's eroding trust."

"OK," said Short. "Irene, I know you're very organized and like an agenda, but the agenda for this meeting needs to be set by your direct report. What you've done is turned the meeting into a performance review. They think you're checking up on them."

"Well, if I don't set the agenda, aren't we likely to just waste time?" Stefanick asked.

"You may have some meetings that don't achieve much," Short replied. "But if the employee knows that on a regular basis, you're ready to *listen* and not direct, pretty soon they're going to ask you to help with things that really matter to their performance. And they'll do it because they trust you."

35 Operational Excellence

Efficient execution of day-to-day school logistics

Having strong operational systems allows schools to run smoothly so students and faculty can focus on learning. They are the precondition necessary for all school instructional success and should not consume a school leader's day-to-day schedule. To ensure overall school success, a school leader should watch a few key operational areas: attendance, scheduling, and facilities management.

Attendance is often considered the most basic element of school operations but is often overlooked as an essential measure of a school's success. Research shows that students who are chronically absent from school (more than fifteen days a year) are more likely to perform below grade level academically and are four times as likely to drop out of school. If a school doesn't have an efficient attendance system in place, it will be impossible to track which students are chronically absent from school and provide them with necessary social and academic intervention. Furthermore, if the school is unable to track student arrivals and departures, as well as their location during the day, ensuring student safety becomes an issue. If a school believes a student to be present when they are absent from the school building, the student could be hurt or in danger, and no responsible adult would be able to help them.

Scheduling is one of the most challenging parts of planning for a new school year. A student schedule must allow all students access to the courses they need in a given year. Clear weekly faculty and staff schedules should be created for leadership team meeting time, teacher team meetings, professional-development sessions, and scheduled teacher observations. A master calendar of all school events should be created and dates adjusted as needed and shared with the school community at the beginning of the year.

Every school leader must do a comprehensive assessment of school facilities before the end of the school year. They should make note of all repairs and desired upgrades and create a list of the alterations needed for the upcoming year. Facilities upkeep and procedural efficiency may seem incidental to the overall goals of the school, but day-to-day operations can easily grind to a halt without proper planning. It may seem trivial for a school leader to focus on school drop-off procedures. However, if the school has not paid attention to morning arrivals and there is a traffic bottleneck at drop-off, classroom instruction cannot begin on time. Like many others, this basic operational event, if not thoughtfully planned, can have negative unintended consequences for school operations.

See also Attendance, Scheduling, School Climate

RESOURCES

US Department of Education. *Chronic Absenteeism in the Nation's Schools*. Washington, DC: US Department of Education, 2016.

DOI: 10.4324/9780429321641-35

CASE STUDY

When Jim Short moved to North High, he made what was—to his mind—a significant administrative change. Dave Gleason had been the school-based director of operations for several years; and while he worked in close consultation with the district central office, he wasn't on the principal's leadership team. Short thought that was a mistake and immediately asked Dave to join the leadership group. Mary Kelley, the assistant principal, didn't like the move.

"I think that's a mistake, Jim," Mary said when Jim told her his plan. "The leadership team deals with academic issues, student affairs, and community relations. Dave works on buying supplies, oversees campus cleanliness, and worries about schedules, bus routes, and budgets. Those are different worlds."

"You don't think clean bathrooms have anything to do with student affairs and community relations?" Jim replied with a chuckle. "Try doing without them and watch our phones melt down!"

"Of course they're important," Mary replied. "But Dave's world is all the practical stuff of operations. The scheduler works for him. He makes sure supplies get ordered. His office keeps attendance records. He's not going to be interested in hearing us talk about test scores and faculty issues. He'll just be bored."

"And he might be bored, Mary, but there are several reasons I think he needs to overcome the boredom and listen to our discussions. First, almost everything we talk about has some budget implications. Dave is responsible for putting together the annual budget I submit to the district office. He also is responsible for the strategic budget projection the superintendent uses to fund us several years out. It's important that Dave be familiar with the discussions behind our budget requests. If we are concerned about declining math scores and we want another teacher, he needs to be aware of that."

"Can't you just tell him, Jim?"

"That's not efficient. We talk about a lot of topics every year in the leadership team, and I could never relate all the background information Dave will pick up sitting in our meeting. I'll give you another example. Every year, he and I spend a day walking the campus. We go into every room and every office. Dave shares with me his plans for major building work, from the leaky roof to expanding the computer room. But if I say we need more microscopes for the science lab, that conversation would go a lot faster if he'd sat in on the leadership team's discussion of the science program. Operations supports everything we do, Mary. Dave needs to know as much about how the school works as anyone else on the leadership team."

36 Piloting Crazy Ideas
Fostering experimentation and new idea generation

If schools want to truly be institutions of learning, leaders should encourage experimentation, create psychological safety, and commit to the regular implementation of pilots. In the early days of idea generation, it is often impossible to distinguish between crazy and great ideas.

Creation of innovation groups like "tiger teams" or the usage of innovative processes like design thinking are some ways to do this. A tiger team brings together a small group of knowledgeable individuals who are close to an issue and have cross-functional areas of expertise. Design thinking requires teams to make critical observations about a problem from multiple perspectives. Typically, leaders want to move immediately to action to tackle an issue. But "solutionitis" happens if cross-functional teams have not stepped back from their preconceptions about what is wrong (even if they are right) and fully done a deep dive into the potential roots of the problem before moving to solution. Problem ideation makes clear that there may be several potential solutions, including those at the edge, that should all be tested. Even more importantly, as software engineering has taught us, this collaborative process must be agile (dynamic and changing as information comes in on what happens during implementation) and put the user at the center of design. While innovative cultures should encourage these teams and processes, leaders must monitor their progress. Teams must fully understand the problem, be kept small in size, work on the identified problem, and not veer off course. They must also be strategically deployed, have a set time frame in which to work on the problem, and document the results of their experimentation.

School leaders must create psychological safety to encourage innovation. There can be no risk taking if faculty are afraid to openly challenge superiors' views and fear career damage for their efforts. A school that supports innovation should celebrate failure, be able to learn from mistakes, and encourage more experimentation. The leader can begin by setting the tone through their own behavior. They must be willing to constructively critique others' ideas without being harsh and should require regular input and critique of their own ideas and proposals.

Finally, leaders should allow for this type of experimentation by committing to implementation of one or two pilots a year. The teams running the pilot should be tasked to preidentify key performance indicators that will be measured throughout the process to assess the effectiveness of the pilot program. Once the pilot is complete, there should be time for reflection on the pilot process, taking into account any modifications that were made to the initial pilot concept and the replicability of the pilot as well as the long-term scalability of the project.

See also   Change Management, Innovation Leadership

RESOURCES

Davidson, Rhoda, and Bettina Büchel. "The Art of Piloting New Initiatives." *MIT Sloan Management Review* 53, no. 1 (September 21, 2011): 79–86.

DOI: 10.4324/9780429321641-36

CASE STUDY

Vivian Weatherston taught ninth-grade math at North High. Jim Short bumped into her in the cafeteria one lunch period.

"Jim, I've an idea I want to run by you. Can I make an appointment to come see you?"

"Not a problem, Vivian. I'm making my own appointments on my phone now. When are you free?"

In a few days, Vivian appeared in Short's office during the fourth period.

"Jim, I haven't been here very long . . . ."

"But you've been doing a great job!" Short interjected.

"Thanks. I appreciate that! What I wanted to talk about is only tangentially related to math. A lot of math, even at the high school level, seems pretty abstract to students. On a day-to-day basis, kids use math to play games and make change—not much else. My husband is employed by a startup that does 3D modeling and remote fabrication with 3D printing. There's lots of math involved in that. I wonder if we could get something like that started at North?"

"Are you talking about emphasizing the math or the technology?"

"Well, both, I think. You can't really have one without the other. And that's the point. Algebra problems about filling swimming pools while the pool is simultaneously draining don't really cut it any more. But building something where you have to design the code and be precise about the physical dimensions—that's cool. Kids would love it. And they would learn a lot."

"The state hasn't figured that out yet, Vivian. No graduation requirement for 3D modeling."

"I know, Jim, I know. I'm not suggesting a change in graduation requirements. I'm suggesting we create a shop class for extra credit where kids can use new technology and learn a lot of applied math."

"Sounds expensive, Vivian."

"I don't think it would be. We'd have to get a few 3D printers, but I bet there are businesses that would donate them. A lot of the software will run on devices the kids already own. And those who don't have them could use the computer lab."

"You're starting to get me excited, Vivian. We need to put together a group to plan this program's curriculum, and we need to think about how what the kids learn in this tech program spills over into other areas of the curriculum. And we need to think about how to measure success. If this program doesn't work out in a few years, it needs to be terminated. It's a crazy idea, but that's why I love it!"

37 Principal Practices
Critical actions of successful school leaders

School leaders are chiefly responsible for student learning and achievement in their schools. Their effectiveness is a powerful lever to ensure a school fulfills its mission and vision. However, principals' roles are extremely demanding and complex, and it is easy for a school leader to lose focus on what matters most. Research shows that three principal practices, when enacted by school leaders, are the most influential to student success.

1. Prioritize instruction
2. Grow leadership
3. Communicate clearly and often

To have the greatest impact on student academic success, a principal must prioritize instruction, or the school will not realize its achievement goals. Every week, school leaders should spend time in classrooms evaluating the quality of the teaching and learning that is occurring. They should ensure their instructional leadership teams are focused on supporting faculty by leading them through regular instructional rounds. A school leader must closely monitor assessment and student progress so the school can adjust pedagogical strategies, design enrichment and interventions, and create the professional-development plan necessary for faculty to continually improve their instructional skills.

The school leader is uniquely positioned to handle a few responsibilities: creating an academic vision for the school, managing the leadership team, and communicating to the parent body. This requires the leader to strategically delegate tasks to leadership team members. For instance, delegating the renovation project for the school cafeteria to the school's director of operations is completely appropriate, but having them build the new standards-based report card would not be. However, not all members of the leadership team may be ready for the myriad tasks involved in running a successful school. The school leader must explicitly develop the leadership capacities of junior leaders by assigning them challenging tasks through the course of the year and then assessing their responses to the challenges.

Leaders should communicate regularly, both verbally and in writing, to students, faculty, and parents. All written correspondence should be proofread for errors before it goes out to the school community. Often, school leaders will write a weekly update or letter to faculty, communicating important information or points of interest. Leaders should also be comfortable with public speaking and should always rehearse and practice before making a speech. This may require coaching, as public speaking does not come naturally to most. Leaders should also be visible on campus, greeting students and parents at the beginning of the day and at dismissal or during school events. A leader's visibility communicates to the community that they are interested in the well-being of the school community and seek to build relationships and get to know people.

See also Prioritization, School Climate

DOI: 10.4324/9780429321641-37

CASE STUDY

Before Jim Short became the principal of North High, he had been the assistant principal at Ridgetown, a much smaller high school that served a neighborhood with 50% residents who had lived in the town for generations and 50% new residents. Turnover among the student body was approximately 30% per year, and faculty often struggled to remember the names of the kids in their classes. The feeling of anonymity on the campus bothered Short.

Short decided he would set the goal of learning every student's name and keeping up with all the changes. If he knew the kids' names, he would set an example for the faculty. Students had a security photograph taken at the beginning of each school year, and Short had access to the file of photographs and names. Initially, he thought he would just memorize the names of the 300 students at Ridgetown.

But memorizing 300 names and faces takes a lot of effort, and Short quickly felt he was falling behind. He came up with a plan and told the students about it in a morning assembly.

"I want to learn your names," he told the students. "Whenever I see you in the hall, I'll try to remember your first name and call you by it. But if I can't remember, you need to tell me what it is and also tell me something about yourself so I can remember you better."

A young woman's hand went up, and Short nodded to her. "What do you want us to tell you?" she asked. "Like what?"

"Like your favorite sport, your favorite band, the job you have outside of school, where you were born, just some detail that will jog my memory when I see your face."

The students seemed uncertain about whether Short was really going to try to learn their names, but as he was walking out from assembly to his office, a senior boy called out loudly, "Hey, Mr. Short. What's my name?"

Students turned and watched as Short walked up to him with a big smile and said, "You're Jim Caro, and I've seen you at the car wash."

"What a dude!" yelled Jim Caro, and students laughed.

From then on, Short had the students helping him learn their names, and Ridgetown was a little less anonymous.

RESOURCES

Allensworth, Elaine, James Sebastian, and Molly Gordon. "Principal Leadership Practices, Organizational Improvement, and Student Achievement." Chap. 13 in *Exploring Principal Development and Teacher Outcomes: How Principals Can Strengthen Instruction, Teacher Retention, and Student Achievement*, edited by Peter Youngs, Jihyun Kim, and Madeline Mavrogordato. New York, NY: Routledge, 2020.

Wallace Foundation. *The School Principal as Leader: Guiding Schools to Better Teaching and Learning*. New York, NY: The Wallace Foundation, 2013.

38 Prioritization

Proportioning one's time and attention to what is most important

Effective prioritization ensures leaders focus on the right things at the right time. Task prioritization aligns leaders' time, resources, and energy to realize key goals. If a leader fails to prioritize the tasks most critical to the school's goals and objectives, they will lead inefficiently and ineffectively. To prioritize well, school leaders should:

1. Align tasks to the school's strategic goals
2. Utilize the Pareto principle
3. Delegate

Strategic prioritizing of the leader's personal tasks to the school's overall goals will maximize organizational success. For example, if the school's annual goal is to ensure instructional excellence and gains in student achievement, perhaps the leader prioritizes instructional walk-throughs with their leadership team over every last-minute parent meeting request. Similarly, if the goal is to increase student enrollment, leaders may want to prioritize speaking at parent information sessions and meeting with prospective families during the day. Impact on school goals is the key to effective leadership prioritization.

In all schools, leaders should recognize that not all efforts have equal impact. Focusing on 20% of the highest-priority items will result in 80% of the progress that is made (the Pareto principle). All leaders should create daily task lists of three to five items and rank them in order of importance to the school goals. They should begin the day with the most important task and work down the list. This will demand the leader stay focused and deliberate in deprioritizing less important tasks. It will also require the leader to work with their team to regularly assess whether the priorities selected in August remain the most important for them in December based on hard data and feedback on progress.

Another crucial component to effective prioritization is the need to choose the tasks most pertinent to their leadership role. A few tasks can be accomplished only by the school leader. All effective school leaders know how to differentiate between unique leadership tasks and tasks that can readily be assigned to others. Effective leadership delegation is thus a critical component of prioritization.

School leaders who struggle with determining what is most important often fall into the trap of focusing their efforts on what seems most urgent. Urgent activities demand immediate attention but can cause leaders to lose focus and be swayed into giving undue attention to less important goals. Leaders must exercise discipline on the number of initiatives prioritized, rigorously reviewing them to evaluate whether they help the organization make progress against its goals and regularly assess if their impact is significant in relation to how much time and effort they consume.

See also   Change Management, Leadership Team

RESOURCES

Craft, Ralph C., and Charles Leake. "The Pareto Principle in Organizational Decision Making." *Management Decision* 40, no. 8 (October 2002): 729–33.

DOI: 10.4324/9780429321641-38

CASE STUDY

Jim Short's father had been an executive at a large insurance company in Connecticut. Short often recalled visiting his father at work and remembered the quiet that seemed to prevail in his office. Secretaries screened guests at the door; his father never answered his phone directly; the only people who came to see him were working on what he called his "big deals."

Life at North High was often chaotic. Parents, school board members, and faculty all expected direct access to Short, often after school hours and on weekends. The range of problems that crossed his desk in a given day ranged from test performance to student discipline to contract negotiations to food allergies. And to someone in the school community, these were all "big deals."

Short coped with the chaos by making sure he started every year with a list of his "big goals." During the summer, he had meetings with the superintendent and key central office staff. He looked for direction and tested his own ideas about priorities with his bosses. At the same time, he met with his staff in strategic planning sessions, trying to translate the big-picture goals into feasible initiatives. And he kept careful notes. "No more than five goals a year," he said. "Three is better! Learn them by heart. Recite them to yourself in the shower every morning."

Short knew his world would never be like his father's and that a crucial part of his job was keeping his focus on the big goals and helping his staff avoid the distraction of all the day-to-day crises. "Remember," he would often say in staff meetings, "sometimes the crisis of the day will take all our attention, but we can't forget our responsibility to meet our major goals." All his staff agendas listed the goals for the year, and often, he would report on progress on them in faculty meetings.

Short was careful to make sure he didn't step into the territory of one of his direct reports in his desire to reach a goal. He worked with his assistant principals and department chairs and coached them toward the strategic goal rather than undercut their authority. "We've got to do this as a team," he thought. That was one of his "big deals."

Watkins, Michael D. "The Urgent vs. The Important." *Harvard Business Review*, March 2007.

39 Professional Development

Experiences that improve teacher effectiveness

Effective professional development enables teachers to learn to differentiate the increasingly complex content required of students in the twenty-first century. Leaders should consider three main approaches to ensure professional development meets the needs of their faculty:

1. Differentiated pathways
2. Targeted instructional coaching and mentorship
3. Purposeful scheduling

Professional development cannot be a one-size-fits-all approach. New teachers may be open to a more directive or guided approach to professional development, while a seasoned veteran might require a more facilitative or open approach. Using classroom observation, teacher surveys, and one-on-one conversations, leaders should map out professional-development priorities and the standards they will use to assess levels of teacher mastery. Once a priority and standards map has been defined, leaders should align professional-development opportunities to these priorities. Instructional coaches and school leaders can then use observation, assessment, and performance evaluations to identify where teachers fall along the spectrum, working with each to create job-embedded growth plans targeted to their specific needs.

New teachers should be paired with veteran teacher mentors in their first year of teaching to support their professional growth. Highly skilled expert teachers should be leveraged as instructional coaches to support the learning of all colleagues. Mentoring and coaching both support inexperienced teachers and are beneficial for the mentors and coaches. As veteran teachers assist newer teachers in improving their practice, they can improve their own professional competency. At the same time, a novice teacher who is confused about how professional-development training should be applied to their classroom can consult their mentor for advice.

Leaders should create school schedules that allow teachers to engage in professional learning and collaborate with one another. Research has shown that the most successful and effective teacher professional development centers around teachers working collaboratively with their colleagues in self-directed learning that addresses a critical school problem of practice. Commonly scheduled prep time creates opportunities for teachers to participate in professional-learning communities, engage in peer coaching, and plan and design lessons together. And teachers who work collaboratively are better equipped to analyze student assessment data they can then use to improve classroom instruction.

Effective professional development requires assessing where teachers need to develop as well as areas they are interested in improving. Teachers want a voice in creating their own professional-development plan and should create yearly stretch goals for themselves. These plans may include in-school opportunities such as collaboration with colleagues, mentoring, and coaching, as well as participation in external institutes, workshops, and seminars. Data from school surveys and coaching conversations can also help ensure professional learning is not disconnected from practice and supports the areas of knowledge and skills educators want to improve.

See also Co-Teaching, Curriculum Leadership, Instructional Coaching

DOI: 10.4324/9780429321641-39

CASE STUDY

When Jim Short first began teaching, professional development was almost always concentrated in big day-long workshops right after major vacation breaks. While this concentration made sense in terms of scheduling, the workshops rarely related to any particular problem Short or his colleagues were encountering in their classrooms. Everyone knew PD was a good thing for teachers, and these were the most convenient times to schedule it. Usually teachers met the announcement of a faculty workshop with a collective eye roll, and their attitude as the workshop began was rarely positive.

Short believed in good professional education for faculty just as he believed in good schooling for the students in his school. Before he began scheduling professional development, he tried to listen carefully to what his faculty told him were their professional-development needs. Not surprisingly, the messages he got varied a good deal. Inexperienced faculty had different needs from experienced faculty. Ninth-grade teachers had different needs from those who primarily taught seniors. Short and his administrative team realized that rather than have a big workshop for all faculty, they needed to provide a variety of professional offerings and allow the faculty to choose their own professional-development pathway.

But just because PD wasn't popular, Short wasn't going to let faculty opt out of it. Short's team established a participation goal for all faculty representing a minimum level of PD hours to be earned in a year.

Many less experienced faculty needed mentorship, and thus Short established a program in which highly skilled teachers could work with less skilled teachers on instructional issues. For both those being mentored and the highly skilled teachers volunteering in the program, this time qualified as PD training.

But the biggest challenge Short faced in bringing his new plan for professional development to life was the schedule. He needed to find a way to allow senior faculty to work with junior faculty and to allow workshops and discussion groups to be scheduled flexibly through the school year. Ultimately—and this took some work—Short built three flexible professional-development days into the school year. This allowed him to carve out short blocks of time for faculty to meet without disrupting the district's attendance policy.

RESOURCES

Darling-Hammond, Linda, Maria E. Hyler, and Madelyn Gardner. *Effective Teacher Professional Development*. Palo Alto, CA: Learning Policy Institute, June 2017.

Mizell, Hayes. *Why Professional Development Matters*. Oxford, OH: Learning Forward, 2010.

40 Progress Over Perfection
Not letting perfection be the enemy of improvement

The pursuit of perfection can sabotage progress. Projects that are successful at an early stage are extremely rare, and there is much to learn when fledgling efforts fail in the short term. Long-term success depends on understanding that ideas get refined over time. Reflecting on the weakness of early iterations can improve subsequent versions, which can eventually lead to a strong and successful end product.

The Japanese concept of "kaizen," or continuous improvement, points to a method by which organizations can get at the root causes of a project's failure. In kaizen, teams can utilize W. Edward Deming's "plan, do, check, act" (PDCA) cycle to create a process of continuous reflection and improvement. Kaizen also emphasizes that the staff closest to the issue are the ones best equipped to brainstorm possible solutions. Rather than waiting until the "perfect solution" is devised (risking analysis paralysis), kaizen focuses on deliberate and studied action: short-cycle implementation of one or more potential solutions with real-time data collected to formatively assess the impact of version 1.0, followed quickly by version 1.1 or even 2.0. The result is that each iteration is better than the last version, as the PDCA cycle is always informed by those closest to the problem.

A challenge for this design and testing process is that the root causes of failure are often shadowed by ambiguity. To get more comfortable with this ambiguity, a team can employ a few strategies:

1. Try to understand a complex problem or process by creating a visual
2. Act incrementally during uncertainty and examine data for directionality
3. Reflect on whether emotional responses to change and ambiguity are hindering success

For the first strategy, flow charts can aid conceptualization and prototype design. For the second, a useful method to make rapid progress is to consider testing possible solutions in small parallel experiments. This kind of comparative testing allows for more than one change theory to be piloted at once. For example, if a new attendance-improvement strategy has staff calling the homes of low-attending students a half hour before school starts, consider testing 50% of the targeted students with the alternative of calling the home the evening before. The team can then examine which mechanism yields the better results. Finally, publicly recognizing that negative emotional responses may arise because of change can mitigate staff resistance to innovation. It is important to measure progress rather than expect perfection from version 1.0. Don't wait until the final outcome to make modifications and improvements in the system under development.

See also Change Management, Innovation Leadership, Piloting Crazy Ideas

RESOURCES

Lina, Lubna Rahman, and Hafiz Ullah. "The Concept and Implementation of Kaizen in an Organization." *Global Journal of Management and Business Research* 19, no. 1 (February 2019).

DOI: 10.4324/9780429321641-40

CASE STUDY

Cafeteria service did not always run smoothly at North High. Every time pizza was on the menu, the cafeteria got so backed up the kids were either late for class or missed lunch. Everybody was grumpy on pizza day. The menus were set by the district; but because North High was the oldest high school in the district and had the smallest kitchen area, it lacked the oven capacity of the other schools.

Jim Short had put together a small working group: Ellen Bonds, head of food service, Dave Gleason, director of operations, and Mary Kelley, assistant principal.

"See what you can do to solve this problem," Short told them. "Maybe the answer is in how the food is prepped; maybe we can reconfigure the kitchen; maybe we can adjust the schedule. It's June; let's solve this problem by September."

In July, Mary Kelley raised a warning flag. "We're stuck, Jim. Ellen thinks she can change the kitchen routine. Dave thinks he can get some equipment repositioned. But there's nothing we can do with the schedule. It's not going to be enough."

"Whoa, whoa!" said Jim. "You've made a lot of progress!"

"No, Jim. Currently, we're not able to serve about 200 kids. With these changes, we calculate we might drop that number to seventy-five. But we'll still have a lot of hungry kids late for class."

"Well, look at it this way, Mary. If your estimate is right, you've solved half of the problem. Let's put in motion the plans you've made so far and measure the effect carefully. Maybe we'll have only sixty kids who aren't served."

"Or maybe we'll have more, Jim. We're just taking a small step."

"So let's think about some other small steps. Why can't the schedule change?"

"Because of science labs. We've got so many kids taking science, the labs are all booked up."

"Mary, I walk around all the time. There are lots of periods when labs are open."

"But the labs are specialized, Jim. You can't teach biology in a physics lab."

"I'm not really sure I believe that, Mary. But it seems to me you could teach ninth-grade general science in any kind of lab. Why don't you look into scattering the ninth-graders into different labs when they're vacant and give that grade a free period after lunch? At least 150 ninth-graders are taking science."

Mary paused. "I never thought of that. It might work."

"Small steps aren't bad, as long as we're going forward," Jim said. "We need to look hard at the data when we try these solutions. We could be creating other unanticipated problems. But this sounds like a great start."

41   Safety and Security

The preconditions for learning and well-being

Being safe is the most basic expectation of students, faculty, and staff in a school. However, safety and security measures in schools are often weak. The three areas on which schools need to focus to ensure safety include:

1. Emergency preparedness
2. Child abuse protocols
3. Partnerships with law enforcement

Proper emergency protocols must be in place to safely meet the need for evacuation, sheltering in place, and lockdowns. Leaders must ensure these protocols are practiced regularly so they become routine. There is, however, a fine balance between being prepared for an emergency situation and being overly vigilant. Too-frequent rehearsal of emergency drills can do more harm than good. To avoid interrupting planned activities, it is important to publish in advance a calendar for all emergency rehearsals so faculty can adjust instruction accordingly.

Almost every state requires faculty to be "mandatory reporters" and report anything that raises a "reasonable suspicion" of child abuse. Those laws make clear that faculty should be sufficiently trained to comply with this requirement and to err on the side of caution. Having an abuse and neglect protocol ensures that any staff member can be supported through a clear, step-by-step process. Usually, such a protocol identifies a child abuse prevention team, made up of a member of the school leadership and a school counselor who can help file a child abuse report, contact child welfare services, and secure the immediate safety of the child involved. The school should never attempt further investigation on its own. Schools should allocate professional-development time annually to provide essential safety training on child abuse and reporting laws.

Crimes like assault, drug dealing, or cyberbullying assault require the intervention of law enforcement. Before serious crimes occur, school leaders should establish a relationship with the local law enforcement agency to create fair, legal, and appropriate agreements on how disciplinary matters are handled. Schools are better equipped to understand how a child's intellectual and emotional developmental stage affects their behavior and when this behavior falls outside the norm. When a student's conduct violates criminal statutes, law enforcement must be involved; but together, schools and police officers can collaborate on what constitutes appropriate next steps and consequences to ensure the whole school community is safe.

See also   Discipline, Operational Excellence, School Climate

RESOURCES

Children's Bureau, U.S. Department of Health and Human Services, Administration for Children and Families. *Child Maltreatment 2009*, viii–x. www.acf.hhs.gov/archive/cb/data/child-maltreatment-2009.

Ray, Rashawn, and Brent Orrell, eds. A Better Path Forward for Criminal Justice: A Report by the Brookings-AEI Working Group on Criminal Justice Reform. *The Brookings Institution*, April 2021.

DOI: 10.4324/9780429321641-41

CASE STUDY

Twice a year, Jim Short scheduled a meeting with the chief of the local police. Today's meeting had been scheduled a month early because there had recently been an armed intruder at the high school in a neighboring town. Short brought his director of safety and security with him, as well as the assistant principal in charge of discipline.

Short and Chief Pendleton had known each other for three years, and they had a good relationship. However, there was always some tension. High schoolers were high spirited, and sometimes, that made work for the police force. Likewise, some members of the force could be overly tough on adolescents. Sorting out these tensions was the reason Short was committed to this regular meeting.

The chief met Short with the obvious question, "Jim, how are your emergency lockdown procedures? Are you ready if there's an incident?"

"We're ready," Jim replied. "We train our faculty every summer, and we schedule a full year of practice lockdowns. We're good."

"I'd like to try a surprise lockdown," the chief said. "Something unanticipated that feels real."

"I hate to go that far," Short replied. "When you rehearse too frequently, everyone gets paranoid. The parents will think we've had a threat."

"How about we compromise?" Pendleton asked. "If there's another incident, we do an unannounced lockdown. I'm worried about a copycat."

"I appreciate you seeing my point of view," said Short. "I agree; if there's another incident, we'll go with a surprise lockdown drill."

"Great, Jim. How's everything else?"

"Pretty normal, Chief. We've had two cases of suspected child abuse that we reported to Youth Services. You know we've spent a lot of time training faculty on their responsibility under the law, as well as how to talk to kids without messing up the evidence for Youth Services. Our faculty did a good job in both cases."

"That's good, Jim. I've got one thing for you and your team." The chief looked at Short's director of safety and security.

"You folks need to do a better job with traffic control after sporting events. Last week after the football game, we had kids racing down Main Street. Gotta stop that."

"I think we need some help, Chief. We can do crowd control, but once the kids get in their cars on the street, that's beyond us."

"Chief, how about if you assign somebody to work with me?" asked the director of safety and security. "We know when there are likely to be problems, and we can work out a plan."

"Good thought," replied the chief as Short nodded in agreement. "I hear the football team is doing well this year."

Rizzuto, Anthony P., and Cynthia Crosson-Tower. *Handbook on Child Safety for Independent School Leaders.* Washington, DC: National Association of Independent Schools, 2012.

42 Scheduling

The real-world expression of a school's priorities

All schools require a schedule to organize where classes meet and when learning occurs throughout the day. However, scheduling is more than resource allocation and operational efficiency. It is an invaluable tool for school improvement. A school leader can create an effective schedule by allocating resources efficiently, improving the school climate, and supporting instructional practices and programs.

An effective schedule needs to accommodate multiple stakeholders (students, teachers, families) while maximizing student success. The leader should begin by identifying a team that can begin the schedule design process well in advance of the start of the new school year. It may take them many iterations to get the schedule right, as each version will need to be scrutinized for its potential benefits and trade-offs.

A well-designed school schedule optimizes the use of time, allowing more classes to meet during the day, as well as allowing for shared spaces to be utilized most efficiently. Leaders can organize classrooms to cut down the "passing time" students need to move between classrooms. Staggering lunch, gym, and library periods can advance equity in access to these shared spaces. Leaders should also use purposeful scheduling to maximize the number of teachers required to teach individual classes, thus allowing for a more economical and efficient staffing model.

Leaders must create a schedule that supports the academic philosophy and instructional framework of the school. For instance, a project-based-learning school may opt for longer block scheduling so students have time to complete their projects and work collaboratively. Likewise, a school that serves older students who need additional credits might opt for a schedule with a later start time to accommodate those with jobs. A wisely designed schedule can provide time for faculty to work on curriculum and instruction. Teachers who work with similar grade teams or in shared content disciplines should have commonly scheduled planning time to work together and create pedagogical coherence and alignment.

A well-designed schedule can benefit the delivery of instruction in a school. Research has shown that students with disabilities retain more learned material if they are given a longer class period to grasp the subject matter. Students who are in independent study or mastery classes benefit from flexible scheduling so they can make progress at their own pace rather than being restricted by a conventional schedule. Leaders can thoughtfully schedule co-teaching partnerships that allow teachers who have complementary skill sets (for instance, general educators with special educators or two different language teachers working together) to support a diversity of learners in a single classroom.

See also   Co-Teaching, Curriculum Leadership

RESOURCES

National Education Commission on Time and Learning. *Prisoners of Time: Report of the National Education Commission on Time and Learning*. Washington, DC: U. S. Government Printing Office, 1994.

Rettig, Michael D., and Robert Lynn Canady. "The Effects of Block Scheduling." *School Administrator* 56, no. 3 (March 1999): 14–16, 18–20.

DOI: 10.4324/9780429321641-42

CASE STUDY

Of all the technical challenges that faced school leadership, Jim Short felt that determining the school's schedule was the most difficult. The primary reason for its difficulty was that time was a critical resource and always in short supply. The time when students and teachers performed regular tasks, when math class occurred, for example, contributed to habitual patterns of behavior; and before long, teachers and students didn't believe math could be learned after lunch. There were always good ideas and new activities that needed to be squeezed into the schedule. And finally, if the school was growing, as North High was, common facilities like cafeterias became squeezed, and the schedule became the means to expand the use of crowded facilities.

North High was growing fast enough that Short decided they needed a standing scheduling team. When he announced the idea, one faculty member told him he had just named the least attractive committee in educational history. Despite that worrisome comment, Short was pleased that a number of faculty volunteered to join the group.

Short put a good deal of thought into who might chair the scheduling committee. He ended up selecting a math teacher who had experience as a supply officer in the Air Force. She was a creative problem-solver and not intimidated by the complexity of how to move hundreds of students through a lunchroom efficiently while finding time and space for the dramatics club to rehearse their plays in the same period.

Short knew there were a number of well-designed scheduling formats employed by schools across the country, so he sent the chair and two members of the scheduling team for a weeklong course in how to design schedules. He also invited the chair of the scheduling team to meet regularly with his senior staff, both to report on their current work and to offer suggestions about the scheduling implications of administrative decisions. He asked the team to report monthly in faculty meetings and to periodically survey the faculty and students for feedback on what was and wasn't working in the schedule. While no schedule decision was ever easy, the new team gained respect and a degree of trust in their efforts to manage the schedule for the good of all.

43 School Climate

The overall negativity or positivity of the school experience

School climate describes how the community experiences the school and how everyone treats each other and their surroundings. Without strong school climates, schools face myriad issues, from truancy to bullying to vandalism. Every school leader needs to consider three primary aspects to school climate:

1. Safety
2. Relationships
3. Physical environment

Schools must ensure all students and faculty in a school are physically safe. Thorough communication to all stakeholders about what to do in a crisis situation is essential, and all members of the school community must prepare what to do if an emergency arises. School leadership should create a plan to coordinate with outside community organizations (fire and police departments, central and district offices) during these emergency situations. To ensure the physical safety of the school community requires the school to adopt a clear discipline code that provides students with behavioral guidelines and consequences for breaches of conduct.

Having meaningful relationships is a key part of a strong school climate. In school, all students should have access to at least one designated adult advisor with whom they meet on a regular basis. The advisor is the point person who ensures a student is attending school regularly, has friends, and is on track academically. The advisor can provide the student with advice and, if needed, reach out to parents or school administrators for additional intervention. The school should encourage the creation of school clubs and after-school activities to support student interaction and the building of positive relationships. Also key are norms and rituals to which the community looks forward—pep rallies, stepping-up ceremonies, and school dances. Research confirms that school climate improves student achievement and is greatly affected by how students feel about both their extracurricular and social activities and their classes.

A school's physical environment plays an important part in creating a healthy climate. The physical environment of the school should be clean, safe, and vandalism free. If a school cannot maintain good standards of cleanliness, students will not feel the school cares about them. The physical layout of classrooms can support a positive school climate. Clustering grade-level classes next to one another is an easy way to build community. However, purposeful groupings can also detract from school climate. Having tracked classes might boost academic achievement for some students but could also lead to other students not feeling capable.

See also   Discipline, Operational Excellence

RESOURCES

Prothero, Arianna. "The Essential Traits of a Positive School Climate." *Education Week*, October 13, 2020.

DOI: 10.4324/9780429321641-43

CASE STUDY

The school's climate was something about which Jim Short spent a lot of time thinking. To him, its most important manifestations were noticeable when he walked through the school corridors. Did the students catch his eye and smile? Did they behave politely as they rushed to class? Was there trash in the lavatories?

Short knew that behind the positive climate he perceived was a lot of effort by faculty and administration. The discipline and conduct codes were used well. The school's emergency plans were regularly rehearsed. The maintenance staff did a great job making sure graffiti never lasted more than a few hours. The school was safe and felt safe.

But Short also knew the interpersonal relationships between students and between students and faculty were the key to a positive climate. The conduct code asked everyone to treat each other with welcome and respect. Short himself occasionally would have a private conversation with students when he saw an exclusionary clique beginning to emerge.

And Short never missed a chance to show that good conduct applied to him as well as to the students. A recent event had given him a perfect opportunity. Across the busy street in front of the school was the student parking lot. A policeman was posted there to stop traffic when the foot traffic to the parking lot was heavy. A tradition had grown up, with Short's encouragement, that students would wave to the drivers who stopped as they crossed. "Those folks are in a hurry," Short told the students. "It's polite to wave to thank them for stopping." And to call attention to the practice, Short told the students, "And if you ever see me failing to wave, I'll buy an ice cream cone for everybody in the school!"

At least once a year, Short made sure he was caught not waving.

One day, Short was rushing to a meeting downtown and jaywalked across a city street to save time. He didn't notice the yellow school bus until several of the windows of the bus opened and kids stuck their heads out, shouting, "Mr. Short . . . you didn't wave!" Short signaled the driver to pull over and climbed on the bus. "Listen, kids," he said. "That deal only applies to the street in front of school."

Immediately, a hand shot up.

"Kelsey?" Short said.

"So, Mr. Short, you're saying that politeness only matters at North High?" Kelsey asked.

The next day in assembly, Short announced to wild cheering that Kelsey was right, he was wrong, and everybody would get an ice cream cone.

44 Situational Decision-Making
A model for making optimal decisions based on context

School leaders must understand situational context to make the best decisions. There are four situational categories that require different decision-making strategies to achieve optimal outcomes:

1. Decide
2. Consult
3. Build consensus
4. Delegate

A leader uses "decide" when there is an emergency. Generally, a school leader will employ this when a crisis has occurred and the safety and security of the students and faculty are at stake. "Consult" asks the leader to consult others before making a decision and is used in situations where the decision would be enhanced by a diversity of perspectives—for example, when a new school schedule has been proposed and the leader wants to hear from different parties about its feasibility. When using the "building consensus" approach, the leader cedes decision-making authority to a group. This is used when leaders have ample time to deliberate and would like to empower others to make decisions. For example, the school leader asks teachers to decide on the design of a revamped advisory curriculum. Finally, "delegate" assigns decision-making authority to an individual or group and is used in lower-stakes decisions that can be easily reversed.

Of the four options, "decide" is the strategy to be used the most sparingly, as top-down decision-making tends to be the least informed, has the weakest support, and often incurs the most resistance from faculty. In contrast, school leaders should use "consult" most frequently. Consultative leaders increase their perceived decision legitimacy through representative input while reserving the leader's right to ultimately make the final decision. Leaders should also use "Build consensus" infrequently, as it is the most time consuming and labor intensive. Decisions made from consensus often result in ineffectual compromises or create deadlocks between competing factions. Consensual decision-making also has a tendency to make the leader appear weak. Leaders should use "delegate" to transfer low-stakes decisions to junior leaders to whom they want to provide leadership opportunities.

It is not enough for school leaders to simply adopt the correct process to achieve the right outcome. They also need to create a culture in which the school's mission and vision are seen as drivers of the decision-making process. School leaders need to communicate that decisions are made to further the progress of the school, even when the reasoning involved may not be obvious. They need to convince stakeholders to adopt the concept of "disagree and commit" once a decision is made and to rally behind a decision, understanding there is context of which they may not be aware.

See also Leadership Team, In-the-Moment Feedback, Innovation Leadership

RESOURCES

Conley, David, and Paul Goldman. "Facilitative Leadership: How Principals Lead Without Dominating." *Oregon School Study Council Bulletin* 37, no. 9 (August 1994). Eugene, OR: Oregon School Study Council, University of Oregon.

DOI: 10.4324/9780429321641-44

CASE STUDY

From his predecessor, Jim Short inherited one unresolved decision that caused endless skirmishes and ill will among the faculty. Two years before Short's arrival, a group of faculty had urged the principal to establish a committee to change the daily class schedule. The goal was to have classes of differing lengths so teachers could have more flexibility. To have the option of varied-length classes meant that not every class could meet every day. Some faculty strenuously opposed this idea, especially language and math instructors, who felt that daily exposure to their subjects was necessary. Faced with a strongly divided faculty, Short's predecessor tabled the discussion of the schedule change and refused to make a decision himself.

Realizing the anger and anxiety underlying this incomplete decision process, Short told the faculty he was going to personally study the issues for the first semester. As he spoke to various faculty, it became clear he needed to consult with as many as he could. In January, he announced he was appointing an advisory committee to consider the issues surrounding schedule revision. The charge of this committee was to deliver, in two months, three different schedule scenarios, with an explanation of the advantages and disadvantages of each. Short told the faculty they would have a full discussion of all three scenarios, and then he would make the final decision.

Short explained he would make the final decision because it needed to be made objectively and not politically. It was clear that in the first iteration of the schedule discussion, various departments had taken strong positions: language and math for the status quo, other departments for significant change. It would be hard for individual faculty members to go against the consensus of their department; and thus, while Short valued the input of the faculty and the tradition of faculty decision-making, this was too emotionally charged a decision to be made that way. Short noted he did not expect everyone to agree with his decision, but he hoped everyone would commit to giving the schedule he approved their best effort. He also promised to reconvene the advisory committee after a year to review the success of the new schedule and to suggest revisions to it if necessary.

De Smet, Aaron, Gerald Lackey, and Leigh M. Weiss. "Untangling Your Organization's Decision Making." *McKinsey Quarterly* 3 (June 21, 2017): 68–80.

45 Special Education

Supporting the unique needs of all students in school

In 2018–19, more than seven million students in the United States received special education services under the Individuals with Disabilities Education Act (IDEA). A leader can employ a number of basic strategies to make their school a success for special education students:

1. Create a system to identify students who need services
2. Convene an Individualized Education Plan (IEP) team
3. Create a school environment that supports the unique needs of the special education students in the school

Federal and state law require that schools have an internal system to identify, evaluate, and provide services to special-needs children. Usually, the process commences when a parent or school staff member refers a student for evaluation. Students may not be evaluated, however, without parental consent. The initial evaluation considers the child's specific educational needs and the special education services appropriate for addressing those needs. The evaluation will consider the child's health, vision and hearing, social and emotional status, general intelligence, academic performance, communicative status, and motor abilities.

If the initial review recommends a referral for services, a team of professionals is convened to create an Individualized Education Plan (IEP) for the student. This team is typically comprised of the special education teacher, a general education teacher, a school administrator, the parent, and the child if they are above the age of sixteen. Parents must be part of the IEP evaluation and decision-making process, and they have the right to appeal should they disagree with the IEP team's recommended educational plan. The IEP should set reasonable learning goals for a child and state the services the school will provide. Ultimately, the process, the IEP, and subsequent services are all designed to meet the unique needs of each student to ensure they receive the best education possible.

Federal law requires that students with special needs should learn alongside other students and be placed in the least restrictive environment (LRE) possible. Often this means a school will create inclusion classes that combine general students with special education students. The benefit of inclusion classes is twofold: special education students are included in mainstream classes, thus diminishing the stigma of having to attend "special" classes. And other students also benefit, as another teacher is assigned to the inclusion class who can support all students, both general and special education, in their learning. Inclusion is generally the goal of most IEP recommendations, but it may sometimes be necessary to create self-contained classrooms in which students with highly specialized needs receive support. Support in both inclusion and self-contained classrooms can include 1:1 behavior paraprofessionals who help the student manage their behavior.

See also Curriculum Leadership, School Climate

RESOURCES

DeMatthews, David, Bonnie Billingsley, James McLeskey, and Umesh Sharma. "Principal Leadership for Students with Disabilities in Effective Inclusive Schools." *Journal of Educational Administration* 58, no. 5 (2020): 539–54. http://dx.doi.org/10.1108/JEA-10-2019-0177.

DOI: 10.4324/9780429321641-45

CASE STUDY

Irene Stefanick was the head of the special education department at North High. It was early August when she knocked on Jim Short's door.

"Jim, have you got two minutes?"

"Certainly, Irene. How's your summer going?"

"It's going well, Jim. But I wanted to talk business today and bring you up to date on a situation that's developing with Robert Boardman, the biology teacher."

"What's up?"

"You know Robert has a son, Bobbie?"

"Yes, I believe he's wheelchair bound."

"That's right, he was born with spina bifida. They did surgery when he was very young, but he has some attendant issues. He can't walk, needs help going to the bathroom, and has speech and reading issues, probably unrelated to the spina bifida."

"Wow, I knew Robert's son required a lot of care, but I didn't realize how difficult the case was."

"Yes, it's a hard one. But Bobbie's been getting support services since he was very small. He's made it through elementary and middle school, and he's only a year older than his classmates. He's a bright boy, although when you first meet him, it's hard to see that because of his speech issues."

"So, what's the issue with Robert?"

"Robert expects that Bobbie will move right into regular inclusion classrooms with the other ninth-graders. He has an attendant to help with his chair, trips to the bathroom, getting food in the lunchroom, whatever else Bobbie needs. And I agree, Bobbie could probably function that way. But when I talked with my counterpart at the middle school, she thought he ought to begin the school year in an isolated classroom and not be mainstreamed until the second semester, when he's gotten used to the new school and the new workload."

"Robert is worried that one semester will stigmatize Bobbie for his high school career?"

"Exactly. He feels very strongly about it. He yelled at me when we discussed it and said he'd appeal if we tried to do that to Bobbie. I'm a little surprised he hasn't been in to see you."

"I'm inclined to agree with him, Irene. I understand what you're suggesting makes educational sense. But this is a boy who must be struggling with social issues a lot bigger to him than his schoolwork. Can't we mainstream him and give him a lot of extra help after school?"

"We could, I guess, Jim. That's not usual."

"Well, we need to get an IEP team together for Bobbie, and that will involve Robert. Let's talk through all the issues, but if Robert remains adamant, let's try that compromise and see if it isn't the best path for Bobbie."

46 Strategic Retention

Keeping the teachers you want

Teacher turnover is one of the costliest issues a school faces in any given year. Research shows that 16% of teachers leave in a given year, with higher percentages for new and English-language-learner teachers. On average, this translates to approximately $20,000 in recruitment costs for every new hire. Of course, these costs are purely financial and do not include the hidden costs of interviewing, onboarding, and training new teachers.

High teacher turnover contributes to an erosion of faculty morale and culture at a school. Teaching has increasingly become a collaborative profession, with teachers spending many hours jointly working on lesson and unit plans. Institutional memory is lost when veteran teachers leave a school. When these key teachers depart, school traditions and events are often left without leaders. Moreover, when these teachers leave their departments, much of their knowledge of the curriculum and expert teaching methodologies are lost as well.

School leaders should be strategic in how they retain teachers. For new teachers, this may mean giving them a mentor who can help guide them through the first year. Additionally, support groups with other beginning teachers are helpful so they can all share their experiences. For more veteran faculty, having leadership opportunities or leading a group of new faculty can be rewarding. New faculty need to know if they are aligning themselves to the school's mission and those who are failing in this task given support or counseled out. Supervisors must regularly observe lessons to assess how teachers are delivering instruction and interacting with students. Without a firm understanding of how faculty members are doing in the classroom, other efforts at support will fail.

Schools that provide professional development ensure teachers have opportunities to learn new skills that will allow them to better support their students. Schools should take a differentiated approach to professional development. Research points to the fact that a one-size-fits-all approach is ineffective. It is also important to involve teachers in designing professional development based on what is needed to best support students and the teachers' own professional growth.

Finally, one of the most important things a leader needs to do to motivate teachers and increase retention is to continuously communicate the mission and vision of the school. Many teachers are drawn to a school because of its mission and vision. Yet leaders often forget to remind faculty of why they joined the school in the first place and thus miss the opportunity to rekindle their enthusiasm.

See also   Professional Development, Mentorship, School Climate

RESOURCES

Boyd, Donald, Pamela Grossman, Marsha Ing, Hamilton Lankford, Susanna Loeb, and James Wyckoff. "The Influence of School Administrators on Teacher Retention Decisions." *American Education Research Journal* 48, no. 2 (2021): 303–33.

National Commission on Teaching and America's Future. *The High Cost of Teacher Turnover. Policy Brief.* Washington, DC: National Commission on Teaching and America's Future, 2007.

DOI: 10.4324/9780429321641-46

CASE STUDY

Dick Brown, the chair of the math department, poked his head into Jim Short's office.

"Got a minute, Jim?"

"Sure," Short replied.

"Bill Scott just told me he was leaving. Going back to graduate school next fall."

"Good for him, Dick. And good for you as well. I know you weren't thrilled by his performance."

"That's what I thought. I think he took his performance feedback seriously, and he really wants to get better. I told him we'd be happy to support him with recommendations, and he seemed pleased. Just to let you know, however, I'm a little worried about Kathryn Stewart. I heard she's looking around."

"That is a worry. She's an excellent teacher, and I could see her being department chair when you get ready to step down."

"I agree. She's sharp as a tack, and she has great people skills. What can we do to hold on to her?"

"Has she expressed any interest in any kind of professional development? I could find some money in the budget to send her to a conference or a workshop. It sometimes helps to get a talented person like Kathryn interested in a new development in her field. Have her get some training and then bring what she's learned back to North High. Maybe something to do with computers?"

"That's certainly a possibility, Jim. I think she'd like that sort of challenge, and I know she likes to be in the role of explaining new material to her peers. That's why I think she'd make a good department chair. I'll have to work on that. I can't think of such a workshop off the top of my head."

"You might ask her," Short said. "She may have some interest she's been thinking about and isn't sure whether she should bring it up. I just had another thought. Any kind of leadership role you can give her in the department? Is she a mentor?"

"No, she's not. That's a good idea. With Bill Scott leaving, we'll have a new teacher next fall, and Kathryn would be a perfect person to mentor the new teacher. I'll give her a heads-up about that as soon as Bill makes it public that he's moving on."

"Is it OK with you if I have a chat with her as well, Dick? Sometimes, it helps a good teacher to think they have access and a good relationship with the principal. I want to see North High known for excellent academics, especially in math and science, and maybe sharing a bit of that vision with Kathryn will help her see there's a real future for her here."

47   Succession Planning
Ensuring the seamless transition to future leadership

The departure of a school leader is a natural occurrence that should be welcomed, as all organizations must renew themselves in order to grow. Proactive succession planning can help avoid the disruption a leadership change might cause. Schools can do this by creating a process for developing future leaders and by taking a systematic approach to identifying high-potential junior leaders in the organization.

Succession planning should address the two different scenarios that require a change in leadership: a scheduled departure and an unscheduled departure. In a scheduled departure, the current leader has planned to step down, communicated this to the school, and provided the organization with advanced notice. An unscheduled departure is one in which the leader unexpectedly must leave, usually because of personal or performance issues.

Identifying a successor in both scenarios can be handled with minimal disruption to the community if the school has invested in creating a leadership development program. The first step is to define the school's strategic goals. It is impossible to understand the leadership skills a future leader will need if the school's goals are not closely aligned to the potential leader's skills.

The next step in a leadership development program is to identify high-potential faculty who can lead the school using the school's defined leadership competencies. This can be done by having senior leaders regularly assess their direct reports' strengths and weaknesses and by having junior leaders self-assess. Current senior leaders must use these assessments to coach junior leaders for future leadership roles. It is easy for school leaders to focus on the tactical, everyday tasks that are so critical to the day-to-day operations of a school. Leaders must remember, however, that they should prioritize career growth in their direct reports. High-potential junior leaders also need to work on leadership stretch projects so they can practice different aspects of the job under the guidance of a mentor or supervisor.

In situations in which a school is looking to make a change in direction or there is an unscheduled leadership departure and the school has not created a leadership development program to identify a possible successor, the school may look outside the organization to identify a leader. Leadership-development programming and proactive succession planning are critical, as continuity and organizational momentum can easily be lost without a strong leader at the helm. Looking externally for a new leader is also expensive and time consuming, as any outside leaders coming to the organization will need time to become acclimated.

See also   Goal Setting, Hiring, Leadership Team

RESOURCES

Bridgespan Group. *Building Leadership Capacity: Reframing the Succession Challenge.* Boston, MA: Bridgespan Group, 2011.

Khalsa, Siri Akal. "Succession Planning: Getting it Right." *Independent School*, Fall 2017.

DOI: 10.4324/9780429321641-47

CASE STUDY

Jim Short had only been at North High for a year when he began to think about who might succeed him. It wasn't that he was looking to move on or that he sensed things weren't going well and he might be shortly moved out. In fact, things were going very well, and Short looked forward to a long career at North.

But Short also knew one of his jobs as a school leader was to encourage and train the next cadre of school leaders who would replace him and his colleagues in other schools. In fact, this was a part of Short's job he found especially appealing. Helping talented young teachers get ready for the next stage of their careers was as rewarding as encouraging a bright student in his classroom.

Short felt that good school leaders possessed some common characteristics. Generally, they were accomplished in the discipline they taught; they had a high level of interpersonal skill; and they were effective at working with others. Short talked to his leadership team about these characteristics and encouraged them to look for young women and men who met those criteria and to encourage those people, in their O3s, to consider advancing to leadership positions.

Before long, Short had an informal list of colleagues who might grow into leadership positions, including his. Some of these colleagues needed specific training, and Short made a point of meeting with them and encouraging them to consider graduate programs. And while Short was always thinking about leadership succession in his own leadership team, he never hesitated to nominate one of his good candidates for jobs at other schools or the district office. Short knew that advancing good colleagues would serve North High well in the long run.

While it often seemed counterintuitive, Short made documentation of procedures and processes an important part of his team's responsibility. When questioned, he responded that the first thing for which he looked when he came to North High was documentation of how things were supposed to work. Minutes of meetings and standard procedures are extremely valuable in the event of a leadership transition, and Short made sure North's procedures were well documented.

48 Termination

Removing colleagues that don't align to the mission or fit within the culture

When faculty at a school are either actively or passively misaligned with the school's mission or are underperforming, termination may be necessary. School leaders often find that a timely separation with individuals is one of their most difficult responsibilities. The leader must make the hard decision to part ways with faculty members who are not contributing to the betterment of the school. When faculty who are not succeeding are left in place, it sends a confusing message to the school community that the school is tolerant of poor teaching or behavior. Termination is a lonely experience, however. Faculty members who are struggling will often protest the unfairness of the process or attempt to undermine the leader's credibility. However, due to confidentiality requirements, the leader cannot divulge the reasons for termination and must stay professional despite the ad hominem attacks.

When there is clear legal cause, such as injuring a child, termination is usually straightforward and should be swiftly executed. More challenging—and common—are interpretations of staff performance, requiring a mix of clear, measurable goals and milestones, progress monitoring, performance documentation, and frequent communication and feedback. This kind of termination case includes the nuanced assessment of whether the faculty member is truly aligned to the mission and vision of the school, as their absence can be a primary cause of underperformance.

A leader should not—and in unionized schools cannot—terminate a faculty member without sufficient notice and cause. If the faculty member is tenured, showing just cause and meeting the procedural requirements specified in the union contract are imperative. The school culture is immediately threatened if the school leader is perceived to have terminated an employee capriciously or due to personal animus. In many instances in which a faculty member is underperforming but their performance is not so egregious as to warrant immediate termination, a leader can allow the person to finish out the year but not rehire them for the following year.

Teacher unions have strict rules around how their members are treated in cases of termination. Whether the termination occurs abruptly or at the end of the year, school administration must have proper, regular, and robust documentation to proceed. Successful termination hinges on the leader's actions months and weeks beforehand. There are often requirements of timely notice, sufficient evidence of performance shortcomings, and a support plan that details how the school has provided the individual with professional development and other performance support over time.

See also Faculty Evaluation, In-the-Moment Feedback

RESOURCES

Baird, Michelle D. "The Impact of Teacher Termination: A Study of Principals' Perspectives" (EdD dissertation, Texas A&M University, Commerce, 2013). https://eric.ed.gov/?id=ED564667.

DOI: 10.4324/9780429321641-48

CASE STUDY

Jim Short met weekly with his assistant principal, Mary Kelley. Today, Mary had invited Dick Brown, the chair of the math department, to join them.

"Jim," Mary began, "I think we have a problem with Rick Southall, a math teacher we hired last year."

"Ah, that's too bad, Mary. I was involved in that hiring. His education looked good, and I thought he might be an upgrade for a department that doesn't have a lot of power."

"That's right," Dick responded. "He probably wasn't the right hire, although his references were excellent. His students said he was often late correcting papers, and he wasn't organized about homework assignments. Sometimes, he left class suddenly because he 'had to take a call.' I visited his class five times over the course of the year. What I saw when I visited wasn't so bad, but his classes did badly on the departmental exams at the end of the year."

"What kind of documentation did you do?' Short asked.

"I wrote up my classroom visits, as I always do. I gave Rick a copy—again, standard procedure. But, as I said, the classes I visited weren't so bad. I also log student comments, but I didn't share those with Rick."

"What did you do when you saw the exam results?"

"I met with him. We went over the specific areas where his students had done badly. I suggested he do some summer work, but he had a summer job and couldn't get free. Then I asked someone else in the department to work with him this year."

"That's part of the problem, Jim," Mary interjected.

"Yes," said Dick, "he's really been running away from that support. Every time his colleague schedules a meeting, he breaks the appointment. Often, he just doesn't show."

"Darn," Short said, "this is a tough one. Terminating him after barely two years isn't going to go down well with the faculty. And I can't publicly say I'm trying to upgrade the department, even though most people know it needs it. If we end up terminating him, we're going to lose some political capital. But you'd better start on a formal performance-improvement plan. I don't like the fact that he appears to be avoiding a colleague's help.

"Remember, everything needs to be documented. Every time you or his support colleague have meetings with him, there need to be written records that are shared with him. And we need to plan performance measures. Midterm exams?"

"Sounds right," said Mary. "Dick, I'll help you on this. Let's put the PIP together and bring it back to Jim for his formal approval at this meeting next week."

49 Turnaround Leadership

The leadership required for radical transformation versus incremental improvement

Radical school transformation invariably requires new leadership. Current leadership typically will be too entrenched and unable to objectively see a struggling school's issues. A leader who is hired to turn around a school will often need to make unpopular choices and hard decisions. Drastic measures sometimes will be necessary to save the school from floundering or even closure.

Turnaround leaders are usually given a narrow window of time to make big changes—typically one to two years. The turnaround leader must think tactically and focus on significant short-term gains rather than creating a longer, incremental strategic plan. In particularly dire circumstances, radical decisions can include options such as replacing 50% or more of staff (if legally permissible and the union contract permits), breaking a large school into a number of small themed academies, or turning a school single gender. When circumstances demand radical action, collaborative leadership is generally the wrong style.

A leader hired to turn around an underperforming school may face a specific but daunting problem at the outset—flagging test scores, out-of-control discipline issues—but usually, the problem is more complex and opaque. Properly diagnosing the problem allows for targeted solutions to the underlying issues. However, while it may seem valuable at first to pore over the data and speak to multiple stakeholders to gain a deeper understanding of the problem, it is important to understand there is limited time for this work. The focus should be on mobilizing the school leadership team quickly to effect new behaviors and create systems that drive immediate improvement. Leaders must not get caught up in exhaustively talking about or investigating the problem rather than taking decisive action to implement solutions that generate quick wins.

Rapid and early success is critical. The school should have only two or three turnaround goals on which to focus. For each goal, leadership teams must agree on measurable targets of success, both short and longer term. Leaders need to disseminate data and progress toward turnaround goals, even when the data is not encouraging. Even disappointing data is an opportunity for the school to dynamically shift strategy or focus. For eventual success, the school leader must consistently communicate the extraordinary circumstances that have brought the school to this point. An effective turnaround leader uses failure and even slightly missed achievement targets as opportunities to inspire ever-higher levels of performance. Ultimately, turnaround depends on helping the community understand the urgency of what is at stake.

See also Change Management, School Climate

RESOURCES

Sebring, Penny Bender, Elaine Allensworth, Anthony S. Bryk, John Q. Easton, and Stuart Luppescu. *Research Report: The Essential Supports for School Improvement*. Chicago, IL: University of Chicago Consortium on Chicago School Research, 2006.

DOI: 10.4324/9780429321641-49

CASE STUDY

Tim Watts had been asked to become principal of another high school in Jim Short's district, but one that, unlike North High, had a history of problems. Test scores were the lowest in the district, and the previous principal had been fired after only two years. Jim Short and Tim Watts had been friends for many years, and Short knew Watts had developed a reputation as a turnaround specialist. He enjoyed the challenge of taking over a troubled school and quickly turning it into a successful—usually very different—school.

Short suggested they get together for coffee.

"That's a great idea," said Watts. "You know how these things work, Jim. I'm not going to be able to talk to many folks about what I'm planning until things get rolling. I could use your very confidential advice."

Short nodded.

Watts continued, "The superintendent says the last accreditation report was a total failure. He wants to do something radical to build the school up again."

"What's your assessment?" asked Short.

"Some of the faculty are really weak, and all of them are demoralized. There needs to be some serious turnover. But more than just personnel changes, this school needs a new vision. They need to be building toward something important they can get behind."

"That's consistent with the scuttlebutt I've heard," Short said. "Are there any senior staff you think you want to hold on to?"

"Oh, there are several that look really good. They're demoralized as well, but I think they're resilient. I've been mining them as hard as I can to understand the school and its problems."

"The superintendent is going to want to see results right away, Tim."

"I know that, Jim. Let me try an idea out on you. I'm thinking we might turn the school into a technology magnet school. This is a neighborhood with a lot of low-income families. Those kids will need jobs, and this would give them a head start. Technology might also draw kids from other high schools. A little new blood wouldn't hurt."

"And it would give you a good reason to replace your underperforming faculty, Tim. I could also see it really catching fire with those faculty who want an exciting vision. Have you tried the idea out on the superintendent?"

"I gave him a quick peek, Jim."

"How'd that go?"

"He looked like the spacecraft had just landed on Mars."

"Ha," replied Short, "I bet he did. The city is anxious to attract more technology business. I can see the Chamber of Commerce loving this idea. Lots of work to make it happen, but that's an idea even I'm excited about!"

50 Union Partnerships

Collaborating with union representatives to advance the mission of the school

For schools that have formal collective bargaining agreements, interacting with union representatives can be an opportunity for collaboration in service of the school's mission. However, school leaders need to take care to ensure these relationships are managed well. Rather than assume opposition, early in their tenure, school leaders should engage with the appropriate level of union representation. Before actively engaging with union representatives on any issue, a proactive school leader should understand basic union contract terms to ensure there are no real or even perceived violations that occur in the daily running of the school. School leaders should know what the union contract says generally but should focus on three key areas that historically cause the most friction between the union and school administration:

1. Assessing teacher performance
2. Curriculum and assessment
3. The structure of the school day and school schedule

Nearly every union contract has provisions regarding the evaluation and support of teachers. And even if the contract is silent, teacher evaluation and training should be discussed with union representation to forestall future conflict. However, the emphasis should be on exploration and discussion, not necessarily agreement. School leaders should be *very* careful not to formally or informally agree to matters not in the union contracts. Under many state union laws, when school and union leaders discuss matters not in the union contract, their explicit or implicit agreements can be found by a labor arbitrator to be a de facto contract amendment. On the other hand, frequent consultation to clarify terms, to understand perspectives, and to give and receive input create a culture of communication, inclusion, respect, and trust. This usually prevents future complaints of surprise and objection to sensitive matters like teacher evaluation.

Teachers generally should play a consultative role in curriculum and assessment decisions. If the union representative is open to collaborating with school leadership, leaders should also consider including them in teacher teams that are reviewing curricula and providing recommendations to the principal and school leadership team. In some circumstances, a school-based union representative may advise the school leadership team—but only when that person is aligned to the already-articulated mission, vision, and goals of the school.

Few decisions have as much impact—and potential for individual teacher complaints—as teacher assignments and the school schedule. Consulting with the union representative on both schedule and individual assignments may enable the school leader to ask that representative to support the greater benefit to the school of a teacher assignment over the individual teacher's complaint.

See also Professional Development, School Climate

RESOURCES

Rubinstein, Saul A., and John E. McCarthy. "Union–Management Partnerships, Teacher Collaboration, and Student Performance." *IRL Review* 69, no. 5 (July 2016): 1114–32.

DOI: 10.4324/9780429321641-50

CASE STUDY

When Jim Short was considering going to North High, he called an old friend who had recently retired from the school to ask about the leadership of the teachers' union. "What kind of a guy is Andy Sykes?" Short asked. "Is he easy or difficult to work with?" "Not difficult," was the reply. "Be fair and honest, and you'll have no trouble."

Short believed in fairness and honesty, but he'd heard stories of union reps who became carried away by the power of their position. He was relieved Andy Sykes wasn't one of those people.

Short began studying the union contract well before he took up his new role at North High. He knew he needed to know it better than the faculty reps and that as he learned about his new school, he needed to be alert to find and correct any instances in which the administration was not carrying out its contract responsibilities.

Short wanted to have a good relationship with Andy Sykes but not a casual one. He set up a regular monthly meeting with Sykes, two of his union colleagues, and two of North's assistant principals. They scheduled the meetings over the course of the full year, not as negotiating sessions but as meetings to discuss ideas, give feedback, and build dialogue. Short asked one of his assistant principals to take minutes, and he and Sykes both initialed their agreement to the accuracy of the description of the meeting. Before he signed off on the minutes, Short often asked the district's legal officer to read them and ensure they did not imply an agreement not intended.

The monthly meetings often were discussions of teacher-evaluation procedures, work assignments, and schedule changes. Short found it helped to get Sykes's reaction to ideas before they became proposals. In time, he came to trust Sykes's wisdom on a number of academic matters and would ask him to serve on faculty committees. Surprisingly, given the time the union role took, Sykes was often happy to take on these duties.

As his relationship with Andy Sykes evolved, Short began to feel Sykes was an important member of the North High team. He wasn't an administrator, but he had a valuable perspective of what was on the minds of the faculty. Compensation and evaluation were constant faculty issues of which Short was well aware, but Sykes often gave him insight into more subtle cultural attitudes of the faculty, whether they felt Short respected them, and how much trust they placed in him. In the end, Short felt his conversations with Andy Sykes were some of the most important he had every year.

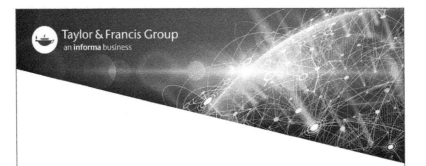

Taylor & Francis eBooks

www.taylorfrancis.com

A single destination for eBooks from Taylor & Francis
with increased functionality and an improved user
experience to meet the needs of our customers.

90,000+ eBooks of award-winning academic content in
Humanities, Social Science, Science, Technology, Engineering,
and Medical written by a global network of editors and authors.

TAYLOR & FRANCIS EBOOKS OFFERS:

A streamlined
experience for
our library
customers

A single point
of discovery
for all of our
eBook content

Improved
search and
discovery of
content at both
book and
chapter level

REQUEST A FREE TRIAL
support@taylorfrancis.com

For Product Safety Concerns and Information please contact our EU
representative GPSR@taylorandfrancis.com
Taylor & Francis Verlag GmbH, Kaufingerstraße 24, 80331 München, Germany

www.ingramcontent.com/pod-product-compliance
Ingram Content Group UK Ltd.
Pitfield, Milton Keynes, MK11 3LW, UK
UKHW031041080625
459435UK00013B/576